Not Too Long Ago

Mirela Gasan

Copyright © 2020 Mirela Gasan
All rights reserved
First Edition

PAGE PUBLISHING, INC.
Conneaut Lake, PA

First originally published by Page Publishing 2020

This publication contains the opinions and ideas of its author. The events contained in this book are based on a true story although some names, incidents, and identifying details have been altered to protect the privacy of individuals.

No part of this book may be modified, reproduced, or transmitted in any form or by any means, electronic or mechanical, including emailing, photocopying, recording, or otherwise without the prior written permission of the author.

ISBN 978-1-64701-038-6 (pbk)
ISBN 978-1-64701-039-3 (digital)

Printed in the United States of America

This book is dedicated to my loving family: to my husband, who has been my number one supporter since the moment we met; to my children, whom I love dearly; and to my sisters, who are always there when I need them.

CONTENTS

Foreword 7

Chapter 1: A Lifetime Ago 9

Early Years 16
All Things Natural 32
The Adolescent Life 43

Chapter 2: A New Beginning 56

Germany, 1992 56
France, 1993 68
Romania, 1995 73
New York, 1995 75
Stanley 82
Back to Romania 86

Chapter 3: An Unexpected Setback 89

Bahamas, 1996 89
Back to Romania Again 93

Cuba, 1998 95
Back to the Bahamas 98
Marriage 107

Chapter 4:   A Second Chance 108

George 108
New Job and Moving Up 118
Marbella, 2003 127
Bahamas, 2004 131
Geneva, 2008 135
Back to the Bahamas 138
Travels 142
Life Today in Florida 144

FOREWORD

Today, my sisters and I all live in the United States. I am here in Florida while Lili and Nicole live in Queens, New York. They see each other almost all the time. Lili is a physical therapist in a home for the elderly, while Nicole works for American Airlines. I am the oldest of three. As I write this, I am sitting on my patio in my home Boca Raton, Florida, and watching my four beautiful children play happily in the swimming pool. You might be thinking how lucky this seems; I must have been born with a silver spoon in my mouth.

Far from it. In fact, for many years I was in and out of jails as a refugee on the run from Romania. I ran from country to country living in constant fear of being arrested.

After all this, how did I finally come to my good fortune in the US?

CHAPTER 1

A Lifetime Ago

I was only seventeen, but I remember the day as if it were yesterday. It was bitterly cold. The wind penetrated my bones and assaulted my body to match the horror of what was to come on that day.

School was on break, and Christmas was just a few days away. Like most teenagers, my thoughts were on the holidays and the two weeks free from school that were ahead of us. We were going to visit and stay with my grandparents for ten days. We had lots of events lined up, and we were excited about our annual Romanian traditions, such as the sacrifice of the pig and making of all those delicious seasonal meals.

At around 9:00 a.m. on December 17, 1989, I was helping my mother prepare lunch when suddenly we heard very loud noises coming from outside. At first, we thought children were making homemade fireworks for the festivities, so I ran outside to check. This annoyed my mother; she thought I was shirking my responsibilities. The noise erupted into what sounded like hundreds of trumpets blasting all at once. People were shouting on the street. There was so much chaos. What was going on?

Our neighbor, a young man, ran into our house from next door, screaming for us to listen to the news on the radio, and my father quickly turned it on. Nicolae Ceausescu, the brutal dictator of Romania, and his family had run away from the capital pursued by cars. The people wanted to overthrow the government and end communism. "Oh my god," I thought. "The trumpets were gunshots!" I shuddered in terror.

The fighting had started the day before in a town called Timisoara. Massive protests and a crackdown from the military followed. A couple hours later, Bucharest, the capital, went up in flames. In no time, protests broke out all over the country.

We were all at home when it happened. My sisters were cleaning the house. My mother and I were preparing lunch, and my father was watching TV when the news came on. It was so sudden and so strange. Who was shooting outside our home? Why?

Within twenty-four hours, word spread across the entire country that students had been the ones to start the revolution. In no time, ten more cities in Romania had joined the fight and were also rioting.

I was confused. With a population of three hundred thousand, my town, Braila, was of average size and was situated three hours east of Bucharest in southeast Romania. Why were the insurgents in *my* town? Very quickly, we were bombarded with all kinds of rumors. My parents were disoriented about the events and did not know if they should go to work or what to do instead. Was it safe for us to go out? To go to the market? To walk in the street? We just wanted to know what was going on. We were glued to the TV. We listened incessantly to the radio. We wanted answers.

Soon enough, we learned that the rioting was everywhere—cities, towns, villages. All were now dangerous. The people in charge of the communist system had been gunned down by youths aged between eighteen and twenty-three. They were running through the streets and shooting into buildings as they looked for ex-communist enforcers. Members of the military quickly switched from supporting the dictator to backing the protestors. Chaos and confusion reigned.

Nicolae and his wife, Elena, were arrested, and on Christmas Day, they were executed on live television with twenty-two million people watching, myself and my family included. The couple were handcuffed and pushed up against a wall, with a black blindfold around their eyes, as the soldiers opened fire. I don't think they deserved to die that way. I sobbed and sobbed. Justice was not well served here. The people who were in charge that day rushed for them to be killed instead of having them prosecuted by a court. Human to human, I felt terrible for them. I knew they weren't good leaders, guilty in the way they controlled and managed the country, but putting them against a wall and killing them like rats? I was embarrassed by the way my country chose to get rid of them. It was ugly. Inhumane.

Their daughter, Zoe, and their two sons survived. One of their sons, Nicu Ceausescu, was arrested and died in jail of liver cancer a few years later. Zoe was jailed for many years but eventually got out.

Ion Iliescu, who led the National Salvation Front, quickly took power over the country. Officially elected the following May, he seemingly implemented a series of economic and democratic reforms that ultimately did little to make any real changes in the country. It wasn't until eight years later that Romania had a true democratic president.

Growing up, communism had not seemed that bad to me. Sure, my parents complained about things, but communism was the only way of life my generation knew. Moreover, the revolution did not affect changes to give people higher quality of life. In a sense, many people in my country felt they did better under communism. Older people who were used to having a steady job and a pension were now left with nothing as inflation hit hard and fewer jobs were available. Under communism, people automatically got a house when they got married and had a child. Now people had no work nor a house of their own. Under communism, upon turning eighteen, boys went through mandatory army service for a year or two and were then given a secure job. Now, with democracy, some jobs no longer existed, and some became privatized for a while and then went bankrupt because of bad management or because they ran out of money.

This is what happened to my mother. She was only fifty. She had worked for the same company since she was eighteen, hand-making beautiful Persian carpets out of wool. She had worked long hours, and the job was hard. Should she use the wrong color, she had to undo everything and start over again, and that could take hours with no payment. Her eyes were damaged from concentrating on the colors. I believe her nerves were also pressed by those carpets too. She was always so stressed when she finished work that she would come home ready to explode. After the revolution, she was let go from the company. They kept just the very young girls, and anyone over forty-five was let go. The company changed ownership, and unfortunately my mother made the cut list. It was a new way of making sure the manufacturer did not have to pay for pensions, medical costs, and insurance.

Eventually, my mother had to pay a doctor to diagnose her with back problems, which had made her unfit to work. At first, she got what in the US would be comparable to fifty dollars a month for her pension. Today, still in Romania, she gets around two hundred dollars per month. My father worked in construction as a crane mechanic. He spent most of his time away from home with only a few days a month off to see us. It was hard for us to be without him.

About four years after the revolution, my father's company also started cutting down on workers, so he was asked to retire earlier. There were no more projects for him. It was tough on our family, but at least my sisters and I had moved out of their house by then and the expenses were more manageable for just the two of them.

Imagine someone trying to live on one hundred dollars a month today. Impossible. Yet in 1989, that was all my parents had for food and to pay their bills. Forget about clothing or things for the house. No way could a family even afford to go see a movie together. My parents still live in Romania today. Their electricity and phone bills, medication, food, clothing, and other essential expenses come to around four hundred a month. Fortunately, they can get by because my two sisters and I help them out. But most people living in Romania today are not so fortunate. For me, as I was the oldest of my three sisters, these sudden changes were confusing. I did not understand then the gravity of the situation. I was seventeen years old and sheltered from the worries that adult life after the revolution would bring. I was still in school, in eleventh grade. I had one more year before finishing high school. I wasn't sure what I wanted to do after graduation yet; I still had time to think about it. In that moment, I didn't understand the impact the revolution would have on us all.

In a good way, it offered many more opportunities for my generation. It opened up the country's borders and allowed us to leave without fear of being arrested or of our entire family being persecuted. I wish I knew then what I know now. My parents did not explain the opportunities that had become available. I just listened to the conversations they were having between themselves and with their friends. They were all worried about their jobs, the house we lived in, the food we would perhaps struggle to afford. No one knew what would come next. Who would be in power? Would things be worse than under Ceausescu? Would life get better? I was at an age where making life decisions comes from following the examples of your parents and other adults. I had no idea what I wanted to do with my life. Did I want to study? Make a career for myself? My friends were also bombarded by these concerns from their parents and families at home. In a way, it was fun for us because we were the generation in power now. We were still young, so we didn't have to put up with the system at all. We knew about the persecution of the communist system because our parents talked about it every day.

They had it hard. There were so many limitations. But now, after twenty-five years, we suddenly had this amazing system change. With this, we were thrown into politics right away. I began speaking with my friends at school about whom I would prefer to be the new president. Just this alone was exciting. I was following the news regularly, and my friends and I started debating what we had learned every time we got together.

Opinions were flying around. Our uncles and aunts and grandparents were very suspicious about this. They started meeting at one another's houses every other day, having animated discussions, talking with their hands. We could tell they worried about the changes that were coming. No one in my family had ever become an active politician, although Romanians always get involved in one another's business. Our family had lived for twenty-five years in the dark, and they felt pressured to do what the system was telling them to do. Now they were suddenly offered a choice in the candidates, but they were scared to choose. Scared because the changes that were going to come would take away the little they had. I was too young to know if the communist system was the sole root of their worries, but I'm sure it played a part. There was so much corruption then. It's still there today, but on a much-smaller scale.

As for the candidates, they were also people who had belonged to the communist party before. Ilie Iliescu was a very strong candidate, but he was a very prominent man in the previous communist party. It was true that he had been arrested because at some point during his career he opposed Ceausescu's views, but he was still a powerful ex-communist leader. How and why people thought he could be a great candidate for the democratic party, I didn't know. He never suffered from shortages of food or water or heat, I am sure. He had a nice house and did not get up at 5:00 a.m. to stand in line for milk and butter. I never met him personally, but he was very powerful during the Ceausescu presidency. Now he was the favorite candidate because of his age. The other two candidates were younger, so he became popular immediately. Most of the people who voted for him were from the older generation, people who knew next to nothing about him. Because he was older, he instantly looked better in their eyes.

I was eighteen when I was put in charge of a voting center. Imagine just finishing high school and immediately getting selected to run a political event with no preparation, no training, nothing. I received a call from the town hall, asking me to come to a meeting with a few other people my age, and two hours later, we were running the voting centers. They put me in charge of ten other people at the center in one of the small communities within my city. I was shocked because I had no knowledge of anything related to politics, and this was an important election. It was to elect the president of Romania. I don't know why anybody would choose me for the job, but I was honored.

There were probably twenty-five thousand people who came through those doors to vote over the course of just two days. We worked day and night. We set up the center where people would come to vote, and when they arrived, we helped them with instructions and information on how to place their vote. When they had made their selection, we took down their information. After, when the center closed, our real job began: counting and registering each vote. They sent food in for us and extra police protection, and no one left until the voting was closed. Overall, even in my voting center, everyone favored Iliescu, so I was not surprised once he was the elected president.

Many people from the small villages were really not well-informed about any of the candidates. For example, one person said, "I voted for him because he promised us three kilograms of flowers and one kilogram of sunflower oil," and then he became president. But surprisingly, he did keep his word. He gave each person sugar or flower or oil to cook for free. People were so innocent, stupid, and hungry. Anyone who offered the people free items got elected.

Years after the election, I was again selected to run a voting station, but I was never able to do it because by that time I had left Romania. I had had a great time running it the first time. I just wished I had been older and had some more experience. The more I thought about how much I didn't yet know, it made me believe that the very first election was not a fair one. That's beside the point: there were many things not running properly in my country at the time, as you can imagine, after so many years in the shadow of the communist system.

Early Years

My mother and her six siblings were born and raised on my grandparents' farm in Gemenele—a very small town of just one thousand people outside Braila.

My maternal grandparents were together from a very young age. My grandma was seventeen and my grandfather was twenty when they met. After they had been married for few years, they had two children. A short time after that, my grandpa was sent to war.

He had fought in the Second World War for four years and then was a prisoner of war in Hungary for three. My grandma thought he was dead. The letters from him stopped, and his captain at that time told my grandmother that he had died on front line. My grandma, Ileana, was left at home with two children to care for.

While he was imprisoned, he developed a friendship with a lady who was a cook. They ended up having a relationship and two children. We never met this woman. I guess when he met her, he probably didn't know if he would ever get out of prison. My grandmother and his relatives thought he had died in the war. Imagine their surprise when he came home seven years later. I never heard the story of what happened when he first arrived back home, but I'm sure that, knowing them, they partied for days. Romanians always know how to have fun.

A few years after he had come home, he started receiving letters from a young man and then a young girl too. They were both just around sixteen years old. They were also written in Hungarian. After a while, my grandma asked him why he was receiving so much mail. The letters came addressed to him, after all. He said that he had no idea. My grandma got fed up with asking him and not getting answers, so she decided to get someone to translate them. That was how she found out that he had two children with this other lady in Hungary. When my grandparents fought, this subject was always brought back into question. I could see he was always uncomfortable, but she never forgave him for it. Maybe she was upset with him because she had cried and been sad for years while she thought he was gone, but instead, he had been having a decent time.

From the translated letters, she realized that those were his children trying to contact him; they wanted to meet him. My grandma told him that if he was going to embarrass her in front of the world with what he had done while imprisoned, then he had to leave home. The poor man had no choice but to never meet his other children. Their connection was lost. I wish she never had the chance to throw away those letters so we might have had contact with his other children, who would have been my uncle and aunt. My grandfather was a tall man with a very friendly face. Always smiling, he had a love for homemade wine and *tuica*, a Romanian vodka. Almost the entire time I knew him, he was always a bit tipsy. Of course, that infuriated my grandma. She always called him bad names because of his drinking habits. He worked hard, but he loved to drink.

After the war, he decided to start his own business. He opened up a company to take care of sheep. Other people began to give him their goats and sheep, and he would take care of them for the entire year, and because of this, he was out of the town for the majority of his time. He traveled in search of good fields to feed the goats and sheep. He had about three hundred of them at a time. In winter, he would come home because there was so much snow everywhere. There were two other men working with him, and they had four large dogs to protect the herd from wolves and foxes. Springtime was my favorite time to visit him because that was when the new lambs were born. They were adorable.

The men worked hard. It was hard to imagine the conditions in which they had to sleep for months away at a time—on hay or just grass and a large straw carpet. That was the bed they had. But I don't ever remember my grandfather complaining. On the contrary, he was always cheerful; he was always ready for a small gathering together to see his family. Eventually, the entire town gave him their sheep to take out into the fields. He would come home every few weeks with lots of cheese and fresh lamb meat and often brought me a baby rabbit to play with. He loved to pick wildflowers and spoiled my grandma and me and my sisters with his love. Sadly, he died in 1984, when I was just twelve years old.

MIRELA GASAN

Even after my grandfather's death, my grandma really took good care of all her grandchildren. She helped her children—our parents—with money, food, clothing, and more. Every autumn she would spend hours making socks, blouses, gloves, scarves, and other clothes for all her grandchildren. We always came over to her house for snacks, meals, drinks, and just to stop by. Her door was always open. She lived on the same street as four of her children, so everyone was just a five-minute walk away at the most.

There isn't a single day that passes that I don't think about her. She had a small frame and large hazel eyes, a very tiny woman with a very bony face. She smiled often, and when she laughed, she always had tears in her eyes. Because she worked hard and in poor conditions her entire life, her health deteriorated. At sixty-seven, she suffered from rheumatism and bad arthritis. Her hands were so bony and swollen that she couldn't even close her fingers into a fist; they looked like big spoons. Her skin was cracked everywhere. Toward the end of her life, she walked hunched over. Her back had given way after she had spent years carrying so much weight around the farm—water and food and cleaning up after every animal. She wasn't in good health, but at least she was with us and she could still keep up with her daily chores. She loved to listen to country folk music and just chat about anything and everything. I still remember her eyes when she smiled. Hers is my favorite face and one that I will never erase from my memory.

While I was growing up, I only saw my paternal grandparents once a year. My father came from Oltenia, a region in Craiova, far from Braila, and it took us an entire day to travel back there to see them, taking first a car, then a train, and then another car.

Hilly and picturesque, Craiova was always more urbane and sophisticated than Braila. The place seemed strange to my mother and grandmother, who used to say that my father was from a different world. People were just more sophisticated there. They spoke differently than we did, and when I used to go there, I would ask my cousins, "Why did they teach you bad Romanian at school?" I would correct everyone's grammar. I even suggested to him that he would be better off moving to Braila, where we were taught proper

Romanian. Little did I know that people who live in Bucharest, the capital, consider those of us who lived in Braila to be peasants with terrible grammar—like if Braila was the Bronx and Craiova was Boston. Nevertheless, I loved the accent and dialect of the people in that region. I loved the city and all the small towns nearby.

My father's mother lived in a small town just fifty miles out of Craiova called Corn. It was a small town of perhaps not more than two thousand people. It had a village center where they had a couple of shops. That was where they sold small everyday items. Of course, this was only if they had them in stock. Most of the time the shelves where empty. There was also a small café and bar where the men stopped by for drinks. They never served coffee because it wasn't available. Even juices were very hard to find in those times. So people would drink alcohol because there was no shortage of that.

My father's mother lived close to the center of town, not too far from where the action was. Us kids loved it because we were allowed to go to the shops all the time when we visited. My grandma's brother was the shopkeeper, and he ran the café and bar; *Buffet*, it was called. Sometimes he would ask my sisters and I to come over and help with inventory or just to clean. We loved every second of it.

My grandparents were very nice people. My grandma was a very strong woman, tall and physically tough. She had a great presence and was always ready to entertain. She definitely talked a lot and was very loud. My mother always complained about her because she was always involved in everyone's business, including ours when we visited.

My grandpa, on the other hand, was very calm and quiet. My mom always said the reason for his quiet nature was his wife. She spoke and had opinions for everyone. My grandpa—his name was Ion—was also very spiritual and thoughtful. I remember him always trying to advise on whatever situation arose. It's been a long time now since he passed, probably close to thirty years, but my grandma is ninety, and she is still standing strong. A bit blind, but she still manages to live alone and take care of herself. She lives in the same home she has always lived in and has no intentions of leaving it.

After her husband passed, my parents asked her to move in with them in Braila in the city, but she said she has no interest. She wants to die in her home peacefully when her time comes. My father makes regular visits to her every few weeks, just to check on her well-being. I often wished I lived closer to my family so I could see them more. I didn't have frequent connection with my cousins, aunts, and uncles because of this distance. But it is what it is, and I don't regret the way I grew up, even if I might have wanted to change some things. I hope I get to live long enough to see my great grandchildren like she has. I know I will ask one of my children to take me into their home when I get too old. I would love to spend my old age with them. Hopefully one of my children will ask. Otherwise, I will have to just pick one and move in myself!

On the other side of my family, my grandmother adored my father—her son-in-law—and though she always complained about him, we knew she loved him very much. He might have even been her favorite. He would drink more than usual when he visited her, and this would infuriate her. She would call him names and throw things at him if he got too drunk. My grandma definitely had a temper if she wasn't treated right. My father was always getting drunk at her house, and she didn't like it. He was a hardworking man, and he did a lot of work every time he visited her. In exchange, she would give him *tuica*. When we visited her farm, she made him work hard, and he always complied because he respected her. If he did the chores she wanted him to do, she would treat him with a drink. She didn't mind him having a drink or two, but my father didn't always know when to stop. He would keep drinking until he couldn't walk himself to bed. The two of them had many fights about his habits, but he adored her as much as she adored him, and he cried bitterly when she passed away.

My parents met at a very young age. My mother was seventeen, and my father was five years her senior. My mom had been living in Braila in a small room she rented from an elderly woman named Mary. Mary was single, with no children of her own, so she became very protective of my mother, watching over her to make sure she stayed healthy and keeping out of trouble with the boys.

My mom worked in a carpet manufacturing company, and for the first few months, my grandparents paid her rent and then gave Mary food from the farm in place of money. My father had been studying at a special mechanical school in the city of Braila when they met for the first time at a movie theater. It was a Saturday night, and they had both come in with friends. My mother said it was love at first sight, and they began dating for six months before they got married.

One night, it was raining, and my mother had decided to stay at my father's place for just a little longer until the rain stopped. She had a curfew from Mary, who still watched over her. She had to be home no later than 10:00 p.m. My mother said she had fallen asleep waiting for the rain, and when she awoke, it was past midnight. She was very embarrassed to go back at that time in the early hours of the morning, so my parents just decided to get married. I find this story hard to believe even today, but she told me that back in those times, forty-eight years ago, once you promise someone your word, it meant everything. I wish things were more like that today.

In the beginning, they lived in a small studio at the very end of Braila. After my mom got pregnant with her first child, they received an apartment from the government because that was the policy then: when you get married and expect a child, you were given a small place to live. Of course, this was before the revolution, which changed everything.

My mom lost her firstborn, unfortunately. He was a boy, and he was born stillborn. The doctors let her wait in labor for too long before they examined her, and she lost the baby. Even today, after forty-six years, she still talks about it with pain and sorrow. The medical system in Romania has always been terrible and very corrupt. It had become an expectation for the medics and staff in hospital to receive gifts and money from the patients in order that they would be taken care of. It seemed that, especially in Romania, when there was any kind of institution involved, the outcome was always tragic. It didn't matter what kind of gifts were given, the entire staff wanted material goods, and if you didn't give anything, then you received no service in exchange. My mom was brought in to the hospital on time for delivery, but she had no money to give them because my parents were so young. Because of this, no one paid attention to my mom until she started to lose her patience. She was bleeding, and when that happened, they finally took notice of her, but by then it was just too late. She lost the baby. She never recovered from it. She was scared every time she got pregnant again. But after a year, she was pregnant with me.

One of my earliest memories is of being in a very large cornfield on my maternal grandparents' farm. I must have been around four years old. My parents had to work in the city, so I was living with my grandparents; there was no one else to babysit me. After she gave birth, my mom had stayed home with me for three months, but eventually she had to return to work. She asked her parents to help, so they suggested letting me live with them in the town. They lived an hour away from the big city. I stayed with them from three months until I turned six years old. My parents came over to see me on weekends or on the small vacations they had from work. I am very fortunate that I got to stay with my grandparents. I loved every second I spent with them. My grandparents were phenomenal people. By the time I moved back to the city, my mom was already pregnant again with Nicole. Until I was around ten years old, we lived in a two-bedroom apartment, and after that, my father got a new apartment from his work; this one had four bedrooms. There was just a little more room for the five of us. This new home was in a different area from the old one, so it took a long time for all of us to get used to it. Our old neighborhood was a lot better because all our friends lived there. We had made many good memories there, but we had to leave it all behind with the new place. It was hard for us to make new friendships like the ones we had had before. People who moved into the new building were just like us, excited for the new place, but just missing their friends from the old ones they had left behind.

Another memory I have from the farm from when I was maybe four years old was around September time because the cornstalks were very tall and ready to be picked. Somehow, I got lost in the field. My grandparents found me a few hours later sleeping peacefully in the corn, but the incident terrified them. My parents told me later that, after this incident, they used to tie me up with a long rope around my waist, like being on a leash, so they couldn't lose me again, but I don't remember that part.

I remember at around this age, I would cry for my bottle of milk. Since I was four already, my grandmother thought I should be weaned from my bottle, and she intentionally left it outside in the heat. I ran around looking for it and found it surrounded by swarms of flies. I tried pushing them away. When I finally succeeded and washed the bottle, the taste of sour milk was so disgusting that I gave up my bottle. Her plan had worked, and I was successfully weaned from the bottle.

In the summer, there was so much dust around the farm. My friends and cousins and I ran around from house to house all day, every day. Our feet were always deep inside the dust, and we never wore shoes. In the evening, it was impossible to clean our feet. We had to use hard brushes to be able to clean them. In the spring and autumn, we were covered in mud again. We needed special boots for it, but we never had them, so again we ran through it barefoot. I hated it then, but now, looking back at those times, I think it was fun. To this day, I still love the feeling and freedom of bare feet in the dust. That's why I travel, to discover places like this one.

It was always so simple but so fulfilling to live on the farm. Probably around the age of five years old, we were expected to feed the chickens and the ducks and geese. We also had to feed the dogs and cats, cleaning up after them too. We sometimes helped by picking all seasonal vegetables and bringing in fresh water from the well. But we did not know those were chores. We just did what we were told. I don't remember complaining about anything.

My grandparents were sweet people, and I loved them dearly and felt very happy to be on their farm. My uncle, my mother's younger brother, also lived with them, and the house was filled with love. They had two cows, about fifty chickens and turkeys, ducks, geese, and around twenty to thirty sheep, depending on the season. In late April, we always had a lot of sheep as this was when the lambs were born. The town was not exactly pretty, but in my eyes it was the perfect place. Even today, I remember the sounds of the animals on the farm and the different smells of the trees and flowers. It's the best feeling to wake up and hear these sounds and smell the scents of home. I loved listening to the animals on the farm, hearing the birds, and imagining they were saying hi specifically to me. It felt like home. I am so blessed to have had this in my life. Even today when I hear pigeons singing or I smell a farm, I find myself thinking about my grandma and transport myself back into that place.

Traditionally—then and still today—families would eat lamb at Easter in Romania. I remember my grandfather sacrificing a new young lamb. First, he would choose one of the lambs, then he made the cut. He hung it upside down by its feet for its blood to draw downward, keeping the meat tender. Then he very carefully skinned the wool. He sectioned the meat and sheared the coat. There was always soup made out of some parts of the lamb. Then a fryer from other parts and, of course, lots of other traditional salami. We called it *drob* made from the small intestines and liver. I know it doesn't sound very appetizing, but trust me, it's delicious. We used the best ingredients along with the intestines—freshly chopped spring onions, black peppercorn, garlic, sometimes even a hard-boiled egg, and pieces of olives, so when it was sliced, it looked like bologna—and the scent of pepper and bay leaves was so appealing.

Easter was always a big feast, and lots of family and close friends would come over to share and celebrate. Children would receive presents. If you were a girl, the tradition was a dress and shoes. A boy would get an entire outfit as well, including shoes. On some special occasions, maybe the boys would receive a watch, but that was very rare; jewelry was extremely expensive. It was traditional for the entire family to go to church for a special Easter mass. Everyone would dress up and bring along their wine and food in baskets to share. Inside the church, everyone took their baskets and put them in a long line on a table, and we would all share the feast. This was always very beautiful—an entire procession! After, we would go home to have lunch and share presents between the children.

We had even more fun at Christmas. Between decorating the trees, hearing carol singers all over the streets and seeing them dressed in beautiful traditional clothes, and eating amazing delicious foods, it was a real party.

For those fortunate enough to have pigs, the real party took place just three days before Christmas. By Christmas, the pigs were fat enough to slaughter, and we would eat their bacon, ham, prosciutto, and sausage. Nothing was wasted. Even the skin would be specially cooked and turned into all kinds of delicacies. We had a huge fire made from hay, and the adults drank lots of red wine while everyone watched as the pig got roasted. Everyone shared stories and helped wash the intestines and clean the pig's skin as the fire burned. It was winter, and this took place outside. It was cold and snowy, but we were so excited that we never felt the chill. Then the family would go inside and get ready for the first big feast. This has been tradition in Romania for hundreds of years, and even now it is still the same as it was when I was young. My mouth waters at the memories of eating such delicious meat. We had enough fattened pigs for around six months of exquisite meals as they reached around two hundred pounds each.

What great memories! That is, except for the scene outside the next morning. The snow surrounding the remnants of the previous night's fire was spattered red and brown from the blood. The sight horrified me. Years later, when my children were young, my oldest son took part and hated it. They still remember in horror how my father sacrificed the pig and it screamed. My children ran away inside the house, calling my father a killer. I hope to be able to take them to Romania again, and hopefully, now that they are older, they might see it with different eyes. When I was young, we never thought about this as killing the animal but as a tradition. It was never a bad thing, never cruel, like it may be considered in the US today. To us, the pig was a rare delicacy. Today, all anyone seems to care about are material goods, and it is disappointing because we forget that these delicacies are what life is all about.

Christmas was also a joy because of the carol singing and sharing of gifts. Unlike what an American child is used to, we didn't exchange material gifts but shared fruits like oranges or walnuts or chocolates, or candies if we were lucky enough to have any. Since we never got material presents, we never missed them. Today, of course, my children associate Christmas with getting lots of gifts and toys. Modern life is modern life.

In Romania, we shared our gifts on Christmas Eve so that we could see Santa (usually Grandpa or my father) coming to the house and delivering our presents. In my house today in Florida, we traditionally give our children their presents the following morning on the twenty-fifth. Yet as the children never actually see Santa Claus, we always have a debate about this on Christmas Eve.

In Romania, feasting continues into the evening with drinking and children playing outside in the snow, along with children and adults in beautiful costumes walking from door to door singing Christmas songs. All the children and adults participating on the walk and sharing the traditional holidays songs wore costumes. The costumes were traditional dress that differed slightly between every region of the country. They were all sewn or made by hand. It's a tradition that these were made at home and not purchased. In this way, each costume became even more special. Christmas carols would also differ from region to region. If the guests who received the singers at the house were happy with what they heard, then they treated the callers with cash or sometimes a beverage. Sometimes, they would even receive walnuts in the shell or warm bread or apples. All this is repeated on New Year as well. On New Year's Eve morning, my sisters and I would always get dressed and leave our grandmother's house very early. Three houses down, my cousins would wait for us, and then once we were all together, we started to sing. We went from house to house and cheered up the neighbors with holiday songs. We were always greeted with hugs and goodies. Sometimes we got candy, and other times we got money. When we finally returned home and opened our bags, we spent hours comparing our treasures together. To replicate the happiness of my memories of Christmas in Romania, my husband and I always try to be somewhere where it's cold and snowy for the holidays.

What a great life I had then. It was an amazing experience to have grown up on my grandparents' farm with such love and adventures—a simple but fulfilling life that I would not want to change for any of today's technology and modern gadgets. Up until the revolution, life was perfect.

Throughout my childhood, my sisters and I would go to visit our grandparents every weekend as we loved the countryside. Sometimes my parents came, but at other times we went by ourselves. Though Gemenele was just eighteen miles outside our city, the only way to get there was by bus. At times this was inconvenient as the bus ran only three times per day, the last around 6:00 p.m., and it was always packed. Sometimes when we went without our parents, we hitchhiked. Can you imagine a seven-year-old hitchhiking with her five-year-old sister in the US today? All alone with no adults. Luckily, we never encountered any problems or mistreatment. Actually, it was something quite normal then, and people still hitchhike today, though not necessarily youngsters like we were. Safety was never an issue. No one gave a second thought to young children getting into cars with strangers in those days, or if they did, they didn't stop us.

My mother's three brothers, two sisters, and their ten children lived on the same street as my grandmother; they still live there even today. Us kids were all close in age and got together at our grandparents' home a lot, playing and eating there. Rarely did my grandparents ever get angry with us. We regularly felt spoiled with love and presents. Our grandmother fed us and just let us be free.

My grandmother's house was relatively small, and unlike kids today, we didn't have our own bedrooms. I used to sleep in the same bed as my grandparents. It was homemade with a base of six long wooden beams, and the mattress was made from old clothes and rugs. This meant that the bed changed shape according to a person's weight. To correct this, my grandmother would have to move the clothes around inside the mattress. If I ever complained that it was too hard, she would make it softer by adding a blanket to the inside.

However, my grandmother did have two rooms for guests, and their beds had real mattresses. This was around 1980, and those two mattresses were made with metal springs. They were horrible. They made noise and would break all the time, and though my grandmother fixed them every time the arch would fall, they were hard to sleep on, and we still preferred the homemade mattresses. None of us were allowed to sleep in those guest rooms unless there were special circumstances. For example, when my parents came over to visit from the city, they slept there. The children were not allowed to rest there when we were young.

In one of the rooms, in the winter, my grandmother would remove the bed and place it in the second guest room. The first room would become the place where she could put her big machine for making rugs and carpets. In Romanian, we called it *razboi*. I have seen these around even today, but only in exposition rooms in museums. She would make carpets for the floor and to be hung on the walls. She made blankets as well. She was amazing. She used wool from her sheep that had been treated especially for those carpets. Once a year, toward the end of summer, the two of us used to go in to the city, where wool ballots would be washed and prepared to produce whatever you wanted from them. They would color it and treat it too. This took an entire day. My grandmother could not have done this alone, so I had to go with her every year and help.

It was a fascinating factory, and I always had fun going with her. When the wool was finally ready to go home, it literally looked like huge cotton balls. At home, she had a small wooden machine that helped her to make the thread. Looking back at all the things I learned and was exposed to in my childhood, I feel so enriched and thankful for everything. I am not sure many children are exposed today to such rich and beautiful experiences. I know my children are not.

Life was very different than to how we live today. The toilet was outside at the end of the garden, essentially a hole in the ground made from very small square pieces of broken wood. You had to squat to use it, and we never cared. Nor did we care that there wasn't toilet paper and we had to use newspaper pieces or cornstalk wrap. Fortunately, there was no roof over the toilet, so there wasn't often a bad smell, except in the hot summer, which brought with it hundreds of flies. In the winters and cold weather, it was painful to use the bathroom. Sometimes too much snow was actually really a problem, and we had to shovel before using the hole. On rainy days, it was a struggle trying to hold up an umbrella if we were lucky or just a cloth or towel over our heads with one hand.

I clearly remember how when we were young, perhaps around ten or maybe twelve, and we had to pee during the night. We did not want to go outside alone because we were scared. In advance, we would prepare a large bucket or a plastic bowl, and that was what we used for the night. In the morning, we would take it outside and dump it away. It sounds insane, but in a way it's just like camping. Camping in the middle of nowhere, though, because camping today has become more glamorous than we could ever have imagined then. At the time, we just didn't know any other way of life.

The kitchen was simple. It was just a fridge and a country-style stove that consisted of a large top with two holes and fire underneath maintained by logs or pieces of branches or cornstalks. In later years, they were able to buy a real stove and cook top run by gas, but they ended up only using it every couple of months as gas was hard to get. For the entire winter, they would use the woodstove because it also kept the house warm. The family room was really small and cozy. We slept in the same room, and in the winter we cooked and bathed all in one room. There was no heating system back then, so we would stay in the first two rooms of the house to keep in the warmth. There were just two small windows in the first rooms, which were not sealed very well. We could hear the wind blowing through all the time, and in the winter, we had snow come through the house on many occasions. My grandma used to put a small towel down to stop the snow coming through or rain.

We had no running water in the house or outside, but we had a well on the farm. Almost every small farm had a wheel with a bucket tied up with a long piece of rope. The water was always cold and never treated. We used the water from the well for everything. To cook and clean, and even to drink. It was amazing that we never got sick from it, especially as the animals drank from the same well.

Today in Romania, most people in the country still get their water supply from backyard wells. There was always moisture left around it, and the exterior walls were cracked and sometimes attracted all kind of flies or wasps. In the summer, I was terrified of going near it because of the bees. In the summer months, it was also used as a cooler because there were no refrigerators. People would drop a bucket inside full of whatever they wanted to keep fresh and cool.

My grandmother asked us to do many different chores through our days with her. As we got older, we helped out on the farm. And by older, I mean I was six years old. We had to pick whatever was growing that season: sunflowers in July; corn at the end of July to early September; grapes in September; walnuts, apples, pears, prunes in September; cherries and sour cherries from June to September. It was great fun, and fresh fruit and nuts tasted so delicious, not like what we buy in the supermarket here that may be weeks old. In Romania, we always ate fruits and vegetables that were in season. Sometimes we would receive food imported from Russia or China or Cuba, although this was rare. These countries were our allies since we were all under communistic rule. Ceausescu let us have bananas or oranges at Christmas. This was only time of the year when we could find exotic fruits.

Picking grapes was especially fun; it became a big occasion for the entire family. The children would stand inside the big buckets of grapes and step on and squash them with our hands and feet. Of course, we had to wash well first.

The first liquid that came out of the grapes was an acidic juice that had alcohol in it, very similar to Sambuca today. We always had too much to drink, and after, we would be hungover and get diarrhea. Looking back, I think we were given too much alcohol as kids, through different Romanian family traditions and products. But the adults never worried about it. Compared to how we raise our children today, their indifference was insane.

I remember one day I had climbed high up into a cherry tree to pick the fruit and I was scared to come down by myself. I always loved climbing anything around me. I used to climb almost on a daily basis. We would try to collect fruit from all different kinds of trees. On this specific day, I went up higher than usual because there were not many cherries left at the bottom of the tree. I climbed higher without realizing the distance. I was carrying a bag to store cherries because I wanted my grandma to make cherry compote. At some point during my climb, my grandpa came home and started to search for me. When no one could find me, they started calling my name. I answered from above in the tree. The poor man tried to come after me, but he couldn't climb up to where I had got stuck. It was becoming dangerous for him. He suggested I come down slowly. When I realized how high up I was, I began to panic. It made me freak out even more when I heard him say that he couldn't climb after me because I was too far out of reach. This got me really scared. Calling the fire rescue to help me down wasn't an option then. I decided to just let go. I came as close as I could to the ground, and then I just closed my eyes and let go, dropping into a free fall.

Thank God I only broke my arm. Straight away, they took me to a nurse who lived not far away from my grandparents' home. She told us it was broken so I must go to the clinic in town. That was even further away. They loved me dearly, but what I had done was just insane to them. I definitely learned my lesson from that experience, and always when I climbed after that, I paid closer attention to the height. There was not one dull moment at this time in our lives. It's a shame I didn't realize that then.

We also had to help feed the animals, cleaning up after them and giving them water. We worked in the fields as well, doing different chores like bringing the cows out in the morning and bringing them back home in the evening.

When I was not much older than ten, and my sister Lili was eight, we had to drive a carriage run by a donkey. We tied the donkey to the front of the carriage and the two cows at the back, and then we drove for about thirty minutes, way out in a plain field. We did this often, and rarely were other people around if we needed help. To our surprise, we never had an accident.

Sometimes the donkey wouldn't budge. One of us would have to get out of the carriage, take him by the harness, and walk next to him. Donkeys are cute but stubborn, dumb, slow, and lazy, and they kept us creeping along. Once we got to the field, we had to stop and tie up the cows. We had to make sure they were secured, or they would be gone when we returned in the evening.

In spite of all our work, we managed to find time to play. We played with the animals, the chickens, ducks, turkey, donkeys, and dogs, literally in the dirt. And we made all kinds of homemade toys. Mostly of the toys were made from towels or just clothes that came our way as well as sticks and anything that we found lying around.

We learned to respect work, respect the animals, and most of all respect our hardworking grandparents. Of course, if we ever did say no to doing work, we knew we wouldn't get fed. Unlike kids today, there were no handouts. Everything had to be earned. We did real manual labor and true hard work from such a young age. It makes me mad that I don't know how to expose my own children to even a fraction of what I experienced when I was young. Our worlds are so different.

Though my grandparents were poor, my grandmother always gave me, my sisters, and our cousins small change for school supplies. She would make us all clothes like a scarf, a sweater, gloves, and socks for cold days and all kinds of vests that we wore over our school uniforms. She would also make things like carpets for the floor or a blanket for our beds. She was very crafty and knew how to make everything.

When I was around fourteen, Grandma would give us small change to go out on Friday and Saturday night with some of our older cousins. We would pay two Romanian leu (around thirty cents at the time) for the movie and spent the rest on dancing after. We often had some money left to buy a pastry or a juice. As Gemenele was such a small town, we felt safe going out at night—everyone knew everyone else. With that, of course, everyone also knew everyone else's business.

All Things Natural

There was little my grandmother didn't know how to do. Everything was homemade, and for this reason I have a fondness for natural, homemade foods. When we were young kids, my grandmother taught us how to make butter, cheese, and sour crème. She made everything from scratch.

She would give us coupons to use to buy bread in town two to three times a week. Coupons were given in exchange for corn or other agriculture produce people donated to the state every year. If you didn't donate anything, you didn't get any coupons.

We would go to a bakery where they had a large woodstove similar to the ones you see in some pizza places today. It was used only for making bread. People would line up for hours and wait for the bakers to make the bread and bake it—the whole process taking around two hours. Often, by the time we reached the front of the line, they had run out, and we had to wait another two hours for them to make more and bake it. But no one would ever get upset by this. We were all so used to waiting for everything that it was no big deal if you got your turn and they weren't ready. Today we all get very upset if we have to wait in line or at a doctor's office for too long. I know I do. I don't like it when I make an appointment for a certain time and I am still there an hour later. I find it unprofessional. I complain to the person in charge about it. If you did this in Romania even today, you would get kicked out of the place.

But that bread? It was always worth the wait. Large and round, crunchy and so tasty, the bread was delicious. I still remember the taste and smell. Piping hot when we got it, it would burn our small hands. Because my grandma lived so far away from the bakery, I almost always finished half of it in the time it took for me to walk home. Sometimes, when I got back to Grandma's house and there was still a good amount of bread left, she would make me *calavie*. This was a mixture of red wine and sugar on a soup plate. I would dip the hot bread inside and eat it. It sounds strange, I know, but it was delicious. And the best part was that we got a slight hangover from it too. Even though I was very young—as young as six years old when I first tasted this—we weren't worried about the effects of alcohol. It was just a special treat on these occasions.

I loved almost everything about being on the farm except the soap that Grandma made from something similar to bleach. The recipe was also incredible. Pig fat with a special bleach paste as well as some herbs, which, in Romanian, were called *pelin*. She cooked the soap at a low temperature for around six hours. When she thought it was done, she would let it get cold and hard. Then she cut it in pieces and wrapped them in hard glossy paper to keep it until she wanted to use them. Even though I hated it, I helped her make it many times. It had to be constantly mixed, so I imagined myself a witch over a big black pot with a very intense fire blazing underneath. The smell coming out of that soap potion was not the best. After we used the soap, our skin would always turn a harsh red, and we smelled like buckets of bleach. But my grandmother insisted that it kept us clean, and perhaps it did because we never got infections.

The best water to use to wash our hair was rain water. She had those buckets behind the house right underneath the edge of the roof. When it rained, the buckets filled up, and my grandmother saved that water to use for as much as she could. Sometimes in the summer months, the water would start to stink, but she assured us that nothing was better than this water. Our hair really was silky and smooth after washing with it. And I never used conditioner back then. It's strange how today I can't even brush my hair without using conditioner, but back then I had no idea that it existed. I don't think we had any the entire time I lived in Romania.

From the age of ten and up, I spent most of my summers working on neighboring farms, but twice I got the opportunity to go to weeklong summer camps. My grandmother paid for me both times and dressed me up to go. She knew how badly I wanted to go, and she also knew my parents wouldn't be able to pay for the fee. She helped me out with the money and bought a few essentials for me to take with me on each trip.

The experience was one of the most memorable times in my childhood. One camp was in the Carpathian Mountains. I had never seen mountains before. The views were magnificent, and the air was so fresh. The people spoke in a different Romanian dialect than mine. Even the food tasted different. I thought it was actually better than the food where I came from. Everything was better here in our eyes. Now that I am a mother, I know that this is always the case with children. Home is always boring, and anywhere else is always fun.

At night, there were four of us to a room. We talked late into the night, and sometimes we would even sneak outside in the dark. We were told stories of bears that would come close to the cabins. We should have been scared, but at the same time, we wanted to see them, and we did. At night, late, after all the lights were out and we had put the garbage out, the bears would come looking for food. I saw a few bears on that trip. They were used to seeing people around, so we were able to see them up close.

On other nights, we were allowed to go to a disco. It was crazy—we were ten years old and we went out dancing! The disco was really just a large room with music playing from a radio. Instead of lights, there were candles to create the atmosphere. The girls always stood on one side of the room, and the boys on the other. Those who weren't shy would dance, while the others would play card games in the corner. This is where I learnt all kinds of games.

Our teachers who traveled with us were nice, so I know everybody had a great time. Every day we ventured on small excursions to visit different lakes and other attractions near our cabanas. I remember the trip we took to Lake Ana. It was the first time most of us had ever seen such beauty in nature. We had to climb a big portion of the mountain following a mountain trail. On the way back, we had to descend by foot; this journey took the entire day.

At this camp, I went to an indoor swimming pool for the first time in my life. The camp used water that came in underground from the mountains, so the pool water was full of minerals and salts. I was amazed by it. The pool was in a large room built almost entirely from glass. From the outside, the windows were wet with humidity, and once we stepped inside, we could smell the water. At first it was a kind of burned, unpleasant smell, and we soon realized it was sulfur. Because it came from a dip inside the mountain, it had healing properties. There were so many people everywhere. Even after all these years, I can still remember the smell of that water. I loved being there.

Another first was hearing other languages. Most of the people there spoke a dialect of Hungarian mixed with a little Romanian. We had fun trying to copy the language, but we were not successful. Every other word was pronounced differently, so constantly we had to ask our teacher to translate for us. This was strange for us, considering we hadn't even left Romania. I was grateful to my grandmother for allowing me to have these strange and wonderful experiences.

When I was around twelve, my grandmother got sick during the summer and was hospitalized for about three weeks. My sister Lili and I were left in charge of the farm. We felt an enormous sense of responsibility. Every morning around 7:00 a.m., we had to take the two cows to the field, tie them up with a big rope, and let them eat the fresh grass. We had to make sure that we chose a good patch with fresh and young grass. At lunchtime, we had to go back to give them water. I wanted to do everything on the farm exactly the way my grandmother would have done. Lili and I consulted each other on the chores, making sure we hadn't forgotten anything. Considering our age, the work we got done to keep the place running was amazing.

One day, we had a delightful surprise. One of the cows gave birth to a new calf. The calf was so beautiful. He was trying to stand up, but his legs couldn't support him. It was so funny to watch him stagger around, but we were both so scared of hurting the calf. He was so fragile. He would try to rise up for a minute or so and suddenly fall. Lili and I were so excited.

We tried to pick him up and put him in the carriage a few times, but he was too heavy for us to lift, and his skin was wet and slippery. Luckily, one of the neighbors came by in his carriage and helped us lift the baby calf into ours and take him home. That sweet memory will stay with me forever.

When we weren't working on our grandmother's farm, we got jobs at a local farm to make some money. We started working about 8:00 a.m. and finished at 4:00 p.m. We got a thirty-minute lunch break to eat or play. The workload for the day was a little less than that of an adult, but if we didn't complete it, we wouldn't get paid. Fortunately, I was a good worker and accomplished my tasks well. We got paid around fifty cents a day. For a child at that time, that was a fortune. I took the job because I wanted to make my own money. I spent it on new shoes and clothes for the new school year. Every year my goal was to buy a watch or a bicycle with my own money too.

I was never able to buy either for a long time because I never made enough money.

One summer, I finally made enough and had saved up to buy myself a watch. It would probably have cost the equivalent of twenty dollars in the US today. Romania didn't manufacture watches back then, so most of the jewelry and watches we could buy were imported from Russia and the Czech Republic. Earning the money and being able to buy myself things I badly needed made me proud.

Occasionally, we took family trips to visit my paternal grandmother in Craiova, where she still lives today. We usually spent a few weeks there in my grandparents' house, which sat at the top of a hill. It was so different to my maternal grandmother's farm back in Gemenele.

At the foot of the hill, there was a large bath made from cement. Inside it, water flowed from an underground river. We were allowed to drink the water, so people from the town always came down with their bottles or jugs to fill them and take fresh water home. This was also a place that women from the town would visit to wash their clothes or carpets. Just a bit further down from the bath, people would bring their cows and goats or sheep to drink. Later, it became a meeting place for teenagers from the town. There was music and dancing late into the nights. My grandparents were not pleased by this. It kept them up late almost every night of the week.

One of my grandmother's brothers worked for the only general store in town, and we, the girls, would occasionally help him out with the shop on our trips to visit. We rearranged the shelves and gobbled up too many sweets. Sometimes he let us help him with customers. We didn't do it for the money; we just enjoyed being there and having fun. We would also visit my uncles and aunts and many cousins on those days. It seemed like we were at parties almost every night. The family spoiled me and my sisters rotten. We loved every minute of it.

On one of our summer visits to Craiova, there was an unfortunate accident. We were traveling to Craiova by train, and we had to change trains in Bucharest and ride for another three hours to reach our destination. Between Bucharest and Craiova, the train made three or four stops. There was no air-conditioning, and on this particular trip it was scathingly hot.

To cool off, I stepped out in the corridor for fresh air. The train had stopped in between stations. I saw some young men stepping down from the train to fill bottles with cold water and climb up some prune trees and pick prunes.

I was intrigued. I wanted to pick and taste prunes too. So I jumped off the train and ran quickly to the trees. I figured I would have enough time to get back to the train before it took off. But before I got back to the train, I heard the whistle blowing, and out of the corner of my eye, I saw the train begin to move. The guys screamed and ran toward the train, and I followed suit.

My parents and people from the train watched in horror, screaming as I tried to catch the bar and swing myself onto the stairs. Fortunately, a man on the stairs grabbed me and pulled me up. I could have died swinging back and forth from the moving train, but I was saved. Fortunately, my only loss was one of my shoes.

I can't tell you how frightened I felt, not just because I could have gotten killed, but I knew my parents would be furious. And indeed, as soon as my father made his way to me, he beat me in front of the other passengers. My mother slapped me. Now that I am a mother of four, I can't blame them. I was only ten years old, and not only were they frightened, but they were embarrassed by me too. Despite this, I did feel like quite the celebrity. Almost everyone on the train stopped by to see if I was all right.

Once things settled down, my parents were angry that I lost one of my sandals. They were brand-new and were intended to last me the entire summer. It was only June. My parents did eventually buy me another pair, but they made me walk barefoot from the train station to the closest shoe shop in Craiova. I was so embarrassed.

On the same trip, during our stay in my uncle's house, our parents let us stay in one night when they went out for a drink. Lili and I were playing on the balcony. I had a sudden idea to put my head into a large hard plastic container. The neck of it was tighter than the body. My uncle would use it to store and pickle cabbage in the winter. So my head went in fine, but when I tried to get it out, I got stuck. I started screaming and got really scared once I realized I was stuck. I had already made them angry by losing my shoe. At first, I was scared that my parents would find me stuck. Then I got scared for my life. Lili desperately started to bang on the neighbor's door to ask for help. A few of them came and helped me stay calm; it would come off eventually. For some reason I was always finding myself in stupid situations like that. Lili was very mad at me for scaring her.

On another occasion, I swung from the street side of the balcony just to attract the attention from people passing by. Again, Lili cried and asked me to come back in. With only a little over a year between us in age, we were very close. My uncle lived on the eighth floor, so if I fell, I would have died. My poor parents had their share of problems with me.

On one of our trips to the small town of Corn to visit my father's grandma, we decided that we needed fruit. My grandparents didn't have any, but I had heard about a nearby orchard that had apples, peaches, and pears. I decided that I could quickly go and pick some from the trees myself. I asked Lili to join me. We took a bag to fill, and off we went. We had to climb a very steep hill on the way there, and we got a little lost trying to find the entrance. Eventually, we decided to climb the fence. We did just that, but I got stuck on my way over. It was a barbwire fence, so we ended up with ugly bruises and scratches all over our bodies. Once we got inside, we were spotted by the man in charge of the orchard who screamed at us. We weren't allowed to pick the fruit there. We started running as fast as we could, and he started throwing stones and fruits at us to scare us away.

We eventually made it home. We didn't tell anyone what we had done nor where the fruit had come from. After some time, my grandma found out.

"Is this from the place across the river? That big farm?" she asked.

"Look how many we were able to get!" we replied, avoiding her question. "They're so tasty. Please can we make a big pie?"

"Did anyone see you getting in and out of that place?" she asked us.

We told her the story. It was embarrassing in the moment, and she made us promise not to ever go back again. She said, "You're city girls! Why are you acting like hooligans?" But in the end, Lili and I giggled about it for the rest of the trip even though we never did return.

I always hated when fall came and I had to return home and back to school, leaving my grandparents and the farm behind. Sometimes we would hide in our aunties' houses, and our parents would walk from house to house looking for us. Half the time it became something of a game as they always seemed to know where we were.

A few times, on the ride home, I jumped out the back door of the bus as everyone boarded the bus through the front. The buses were always packed with people; it took my father a few moments before realizing I was gone. He was furious when I did that. One time he beat me so badly bystanders attempted to hit *him* to make him stop. The town was small, and word soon spread about me escaping the bus.

When we got home, I felt so stuck in our apartment. My parents fought over anything and everything, and the house took on a depressing atmosphere. I would cry and protest about how much I hated being home, but it did me no good as my father hated the drama and ignored my complaints.

When I turned eight, I had a fight with my parents on a Monday after school. Instead of staying home, I went straight to my grandparents. My grandparents lived an hour away, and it was really hard to get there. They didn't have a phone, my parents didn't know I was there, and by evening they had started to panic. They called someone who lived close to my grandparents in Gemenele to find out if I was there. It was the only place I could have been. As the next day was Tuesday and a school day, they wanted to make sure that I got back to the city on time to go to school. I was also only eight; I was very young. When my grandparents heard that my parents had called, they got hold of a phone to talk with my parents about me. My grandma told them that they should be ashamed of themselves about how they were behaving inside the house. She said, "If you don't make sure you both get help, I will take care of your children here in Gemenele myself."

My parents knew she wasn't joking, so they promised her that they would change. Unfortunately, just a week later, the drama continued again with my parents. Truthfully, they have never really stopped.

I wouldn't leave Gemenele unless my grandma walked me to school in the morning and then took me to my parents' house and made them promise not to beat me for running away. She stayed for two nights to make sure they would leave me alone. The small town now knew who I was because of my attempts to escape the bus to Braila, and everyone knew the love I had for my grandparents. Every time I ran away, I went to Gemenele, straight to my grandparents.

My grandmother was so good to me. Even when she wasn't called to intervene in my fights with my parents, she would surprise me and come to school, wait for me to finish, and take me out on a small shopping spree. When I was six and in the first grade, my grandmother bought me my first watch. It was round and small with a white face inside and gold bracelet. I loved it like I loved her and wore it with pride.

When I was twelve, my maternal grandfather fell off a ladder and his hernia burst. By the time he got to the hospital, he had developed an infection and died. The big hospital was one hour away by car. Our family didn't own a car; we depended on other people to drive us. Having a car was a luxury then. We didn't have phones either. It had been almost a full day before we managed to get my grandfather in to be seen. By that time, it was too late.

His death was so sudden and such a tragedy. My uncles washed him and dressed him in his best clothes and laid him out for two nights in the main room, which was traditional practice. After two days, everyone came by to pay their respects to him and my grandma. Grandma cooked for everyone and prepared drinks as everyone shared their stories about him.

The coffin was open, as is Romanian tradition, and some people touched his face and hands; others lay on his chest openly sobbing.

All this was very moving for us kids. Even today I don't like going to funerals, but as a kid it was scary to watch.

Because of these traditions in Romania at the time, I eventually got used to funeral processions. A short while after my grandfather passed, one of my cousins (who was just four years old) died from third-degree burns. His mother was cooking in a big pot on the stove, and he was hungry. He tried to get some food out of the pot, and the entire pot fell over his small body. He made it to the hospital but died a few hours later.

Before my cousin died, I was able to see him in the hospital. I will never forget that sad sight and how much pain the poor child was in. He asked me to give him some water to drink, but the nurses forbade it. I was around ten years old at this time. It was dreadful to see him there and not be allowed to help him. I just had to leave the room knowing that I might never see him again. His death was a tragedy for the entire town. It had been such a stupid accident. My grandmother was especially distressed from losing her grandson, and even more so soon after losing my grandfather. My cousin had spent a lot time with her on the farm, and she loved him dearly. His parents lived in the same town, just a short walking distance away, and they left him in the care of my grandparents many times.

After my grandfather's death, my grandma felt lost for a while. She didn't know what she wanted to do with the farm now that she had to take care of it on her own. She was just sixty-eight years old. She did manage to do the work herself, but eventually she let go of some of the animals and little by little just kept the ones necessary for her.

Rarely did she come to the city to stay at our apartment. She used to say, "Who is going to watch my farm while I am away? No one will stop by to feed my animals and water the plants." We always loved to have her visit us and to spoil her for a bit with the bustle of city life. We wanted to help her take a break from all the work on the farm.

When she did come to the city, she loved it. Her favorite thing to do was to take a bath—a luxury for her as there were no baths on the farm. Having always been frugal, she would only put a bit of water in the bottom of the tub. She used to say she will drown if it's too much. This always made us laugh.

Another thing we liked to do with her was to take her to the biggest general shop we had in town that sold all kinds of items, like clothing, shoes, electronics, and furniture. She was always afraid to go on the escalator. I used to hold her by the hand and force her to go up. Once she had both feet on the step, her fear faded, and she enjoyed it. But just getting her to do that was a task every time.

In many ways, modern life was a real treat for her. She loved to watch TV and listen to country music; it made her sob and we felt bad seeing her sad. She was one of those few people who could laugh and cry at the same time when she was happy. Every evening before she went to bed, she would tell us stories of real events, and she was a great storyteller. I remember her telling me about her life when she was much younger, when her children were babies. This was when my grandfather was away at war. All of her six children were very young, and she was left with them and the farm. She couldn't work another job to make money because she had to run the farm. Her children all helped her with the chores where they could. This was how the way life was in rural Romania.

The Adolescent Life

My sisters and I were always very close. We had many fights when we were younger—especially Lili and I—but Nicole and I always got along well. We went through many accidents that almost killed us all. I remember one summer we decided we wanted to go out swimming. It was a beautiful hot day on our summer break, but none of us knew how to swim. The blue Danube ran through our city, so we actually had the opportunity to swim in the summers if we wanted. My parents never took time to teach us how to swim. I guess it was not on their list of priorities. So the three of us went to the beach.

We had found a small fisherman's boat tied up to the shore. It was not ours, but to show off, I told my sisters that we would use it for fun anyway. There was no one around to watch us, so I dragged the tiny boat to the shore and helped my sisters to get in. I was just about twelve at the most, perhaps a little younger, and Nicole was not more than four years old. As I tried to get myself in, the current pushed the boat away from the shore. I found myself now hanging with my head on the boat and the rest of my body in the water. I had struggled to lift myself into the boat as well, but I just couldn't do it. I was not strong enough. My sisters screamed at me to get in, and at the same time, they yelled at anyone passing by to help us. The boat had moved quite a good way into the water, and my efforts to get in pushed it out even more. I slid down a few times; I could not hold myself up anymore. Eventually someone passed by and pulled the small boat to the shore. No one really cared whose boat it was or why we were in it.

Another time, we were playing close to the shore with an inflatable donut. Suddenly, the air came out of it, and the three of us were fighting for our lives again. A passerby realized that we were actually screaming because we were in distress and came to get us out. I only remember fighting for our lives in this moment; it's all a blur. I eventually learned how to swim when I was thirty years old.

High school always seems to be an interesting time in any young person's life, and as I approached this stage, things got better for me. Not only did I make new friends, but in ninth grade I found Laura, my one very best friend at the time.

By the time I got to high school, I was a tomboy and the most feared girl in my classroom. I went to a lyceum—a kind of high school—to study construction and architecture, something not considered cool for a girl. But because my grades had been poor in grade school, I was left with only a few choices for high school. The school system is different to the one we have here in the US. I had to get good grades to attend certain schools, and I could only retake a few subjects in the summer before high school, so by the time I had worked to improve my grades, the lyceum I chose was the best option I could be accepted into in my city. It wasn't the best of them all, but it was better than if I had to retake my exams.

There were only six girls in the classroom and thirty boys. That was when I meet my best friend Laura. We liked each other right away, so the two of us became inseparable. I was not a great student as I was too busy to study. My mother kept us occupied with different chores when we were home. She didn't care about school. She didn't consider me very intelligent and told me that I would still be an idiot whether I studied or not. I care deeply for my parents, but for many years I had trouble loving them. As I grew older, I learned not to let their comments bother me. Now that I am a mother myself, and because of conversations I had with her, I feel my mom was just very stressed at the time.

Living in a communistic system, and with my father always traveling for work, life was hard on my mother. Taking care of three girls was not easy. On top of this, she had a full-time job to make more money for food and to buy us what we needed. She was angry at her situation. Angry that she had us. Always miserable and depressed, and she blamed us for everything. It was tough, but I can understand why and I appreciate all that she did for us despite her struggle. I wish times had been different and some of my memories of my childhood could have been happier ones, but unfortunately this was not so.

Every year, school started on September 15. Part of the school regulations for the students was to do field work. At the beginning of the school year, we had no class for the first month. Instead, we were credited for going into the fields every day from 7:30 a.m. until 5:00 or 6:00 p.m. and collecting crops and whatever the school needed in produce. That was part of how the communist system worked; they used students and soldiers for work. All of us were graded for our behavior in the fields and how hard we worked. We were taken out to different towns almost every day. We picked different fruits or vegetables, from corn to strawberries, tomatoes, onions, peppers. We had to bring lunch and snacks for ourselves, along with water. They gave us nothing from the state. I always tried to snatch away whatever we picked that day and take some home. Sometimes they let us do that, but most of the times we got checked just before we walked back to the bus, and they would take everything out of our bags. I always hated when that happened. My mother insisted I always try smuggling what we picked to bring it back home. She got so used to it that whenever I came home empty-handed, she would give me a hard time. The best part of the entire experience was that we always created beautiful friendships that lasted the rest of the year. There was a lot of bonding on those trips. We were seated together on the buses, and knowing who you would sit with at lunchtime was a major thing for us high schoolers. It definitely helped us connect better before the school year started.

In August, still on vacation, we still had to meet up for an entire week and practice. The entire country was expected to show respect for Ceausescu on his birthday, August 23, by celebrating and marching out in the streets. We gathered in the city's stadium every day, putting together a show for him, carrying large cards, and performing different marches and songs.

A dear friend of mine, who lived in Bucharest at the time, told me that she was chosen by her teachers as one of the children to give him flowers and a hug for three years in a row. Before giving him the flowers, the children were scrutinized. Their hands and arms had to be thoroughly cleaned well before touching him. Watched carefully by his security guards, the kids were told to stay as far away from him as possible and not to breathe near him. She hated it but had no choice but to do what she was asked. It was mandatory to show up. Unless you were sick and you brought a letter from your doctor, you couldn't miss it. If you happened to miss the event with no approval from a doctor, then you were made to repeat your entire school year. The actions taken to punish this absence were just insane. Not just for the event itself, but also for those children who didn't behave during the week's rehearsal. It was around three hours or more of rehearsal time daily. The problem was that if you didn't pay attention to the directions, then whatever message we were trying to create on our cards would get all messed up. Each individual had to write perfectly. Ceausescu never showed up to any of the presentations we did, but the entire town hall was there, as were the big shots from the army, so we really did the procession for them. On that day, if you were to watch TV, it was all that was shown, the entire country celebrating one man's birthday. None of my friends were able to travel during this time of summer. What a strange way to meet up again just before school started over.

As a teenager, nothing excited me more than the dances held on Friday and Saturday night. They usually had live music. We all wore our best clothes, and as everyone was in a great mood, fights rarely broke out, or at least I never saw one. I attended my first dance at fourteen and met my first boyfriend there.

Most of us were young, between fourteen and twenty, but sometimes older people came to watch us dance and to see who was dancing with whom. I always wished that my grandma had come to watch, but unfortunately she lived too far away. By word of mouth, somehow, she always knew who I had danced with and what had happened the entire time I was out.

During these summer months, I left the house around 7:00 p.m. and started the evening with a quick stop at the café to buy something sweet. After that, I would go to the small cinema that we had in town. Sometimes if there was no movie to watch, they would show a small musical instead. When the show was over, it would be around 10:00 p.m. and time for the disco dancing to open. I would get home around midnight or just shortly after, once the dancing had ended. I did this with one of my cousins who lived near my grandma or with the daughter of my godmother, who was just three years older than me. Just a few times I went alone, but I would always make new friends by the end of the night. I am not naturally a shy person, and I wouldn't want to stay home just because I had no one to go out with. Most of the time I had no choice but to walk home alone because, although I wanted to go out, I didn't want to be there until the early hours of the next morning.

On the occasion that there were no adults to pick us up, we had to walk back home alone, and for me this was a three-mile walk. There were no streetlights, and it was completely dark. Nor did I ever see any police patrolling the streets. At the same time, unpaved roads made it challenging to walk without falling.

Naturally I felt afraid to walk home and always tried to walk with a male friend. My cousins were supposed to watch over me, but busy with their friends, they would forget. In general, we didn't have the kinds of fears people have today of being attacked and robbed by others if out alone at night. I wasn't afraid of getting attacked by people—in a town of two thousand people or so, everyone knew one another, and we felt safe. But I was afraid of outside terrors. There were a lot of things to be scared of outside during those days. Even now there are still wild dogs that live on the streets. Once in a while we would hear terrible stories of people getting attacked, so to get home faster, I would take off my shoes and run, just in case. A few times, I did get chased and had to ward off the dogs by throwing my shoes at them.

In Romania at the time, there was a lot of pressure on young women to get married by the time she reached twenty. For boys, the age was a little later, around twenty-four or twenty-five. After knowing my boyfriend, Adrian, for only a year, it was the natural thing that we got married. It was in November 1990, when I was just eighteen. I was still in high school, but I married him anyway because I was desperate to leave my parents' house. They were always strict, and I realized they were very unhappy people. At home the atmosphere was more depressing than it was fun. It was never good, no matter how much my sisters and I tried, and our parents worked us hard all the time. Despite this, we were still bad girls. I decided to get out of their house, and getting married sounded like an opportunity for freedom. I didn't realize at the time that I was actually tying myself up even more. This time to a man.

I was trying, but I had not graduated from high school as I was forced to repeat a grade due to an unfortunate incident that happened when I was sixteen. I had an ugly fight with my technology teacher. He had asked me to go out with him, even though he was my teacher and he was twenty-eight years old. I knew that he liked me from school. He always wore a strange little smile on his face. I thought it was odd for him to invite me out, but I was in bad shape in his class, so I thought perhaps it might help me to improve my grade by being nice to him. I went out with him for a juice, and he made a move on me. When I realized his intentions, I refused him and left him at the little café-bar. Furious, he told me he would give me a hard time in school. Stupidly, I didn't go to the school director and report him as I was afraid no one would believe my word against a teacher's.

    I started to skip his classes. He failed me, and I had to repeat the tenth grade. My parents were very embarrassed. It was very unheard of for a girl to repeat the school year. My parents never knew the reason for it. They considered me to be stupid, and that was it. I felt humiliated, especially when I returned in September and I was now in the grade below my old classmates and friends. Everyone was in eleventh grade, and I was still in tenth. It took me a very long time to accept it and move on, perhaps longer than it should have. In the beginning, a few people made some nasty comments, but I just pretended I didn't hear them. I soon discovered there was also another guy who had gone through the same experience and was in the same grade as me, and lots of people feared him.

    After that, the beginnings of any bullying died quickly. It was that same year I also met my Adrian. It was just shortly after my birthday, June 20, that I decided I wanted to get married. I had a birthday party for the first time at my parents' house. There were about ten boys and girls there, and I can still to this day remember what I was wearing. It was a beautiful blue mini dress. I was very thin, with long blond hair and blue eyes. My boyfriend was invited to that party too. He was eight years older than me, so he didn't exactly fit in with everyone else there. I remember my mom asking me "Who's the guy?" and when I said "My boyfriend," she was not happy with me.

    Shortly after the party, Adrian came over to the house and told my parents about our plans for the future. His mother and father came too. From the very start, it was a serious conversation. I felt trapped in my parents' house, and I was exploring what it meant to be eighteen, so I felt that marriage was the next step for me. I agree totally with my parents now. Of course, it was far too soon for me to get married at eighteen, but I didn't want to hear that then. Even though they were right, I wish they had discussed it with me instead of screaming at me and calling me names. Because of their attitude, I told them our minds were made up and I was moving out of my parents' home to live with Adrian in his parents' house. My parents told us that they had no money to help us start our new life. Because I was just eighteen, they were not yet prepared for me to move out, so there was little money to spare. Adrian and I told them that it doesn't matter; we would make it work ourselves. There was a lot we didn't know then. I wish I had listened.

My parents were very upset that I had not waited to finish school before I got married. I told them not to worry, and that I would still finish school. But after about six months into my marriage, I stopped attending. It was unusual to be married and still going to high school, and some of my friends and even teachers were making fun of me. Again, they were right; I was making bad decisions. I learned that years later. It was twelve years later when I finally got my GED in New York.

My husband was eight years older than me, and he was charming and intelligent. I felt lucky to have married him. He spoke three languages and knew how to make a fast buck. He had many important friends, most of them gangsters of the revolution like him.

But he was also very Romanian: he could sometimes get possessive, jealous, and invidious—so could we all. But this caused friction between us as I was outspoken, and he would be quick to get angry at me for not being a compliant wife. And so a few months later, I regretted marrying him. It was not what I thought married life would be like. I did have freedom from my parents, but now I was tied to a husband.

Marriage can change people too. His family became overbearing, too, and I had to be around them constantly. Most of them were nice, but still I was not used to answering to everyone. He loved his family, and I could never complain or talk about any of them with him. Opening up to him was not possible. It was not in our nature to actually sit down and discuss when problems arose, so we just ignored the issues to get on with whatever life threw at us. It was a very different culture than in the US.

If I told my parents that I was not happy, I knew they would make my life a misery. I had to bottle it up inside me. At that time in Romania, divorce was shameful. Even if I could have divorced him, my parents, who had been displeased when I told them I wanted to get married, would not have welcomed me back into their house.

We lived with his parents and sister in a four-bedroom house. His parents had two bedrooms, his sister had one, and although she got married a year later, she continued living in that one bedroom. She stayed in the same house with my mother-in-law even after having two sons. It's funny to me that she still lives there today. Her children both live in the US now, but she is in the same house with her mom. Nothing has changed. Some people can live just fine that way. I knew it wasn't for me.

We had one bedroom and one living area and made ourselves a small kitchenette outside in a hallway. I was claustrophobic, and to make things worse, the house was in poor condition. The bathroom, a horrible room with a very old toilet, was down a long hallway. Having come from a scrupulously clean four-bedroom apartment with two modern bathrooms and showers, this bothered me even though it didn't bother Adrian's family.

The house had no running water, not even a sink. To cook, we used a small portable gas tank when we had access. It was difficult to refill it when it ran out, so we had to be conscious of how much we used. To wash, we had to carry water upstairs in a bucket from a floor below. The water was cold, so once we got upstairs, we had to warm it up. That was always a debate between us because we wanted to save the gas just for cooking, but we wanted to be warm too. These living conditions made me bitterly unhappy, and I would go to my parents' house a few times a week just to wash and feel relief from the pressures of living there.

I felt like I had moved from the city into the country, and instead of moving up, I had moved down. Over time, I did learn to get used to these conditions. It upset me very much that Adrian and I were not able to communicate about us and our living arrangements. My grandma gave us a bed to sleep on and some sheets to cover it. We really started from nothing. Perhaps if we could have learned to open up to each other, this would have helped our relationship. Every time I made even the slightest comment on how I didn't like the way we lived, he would get defensive and we would argue. I was unhappy and learned to keep all my thoughts deep inside me. I couldn't talk about it with my parents because right away they would say "I told you so," and I could never tell his parents what I thought. They had lived in that house for most of their lives, and they loved it. In their eyes, there was nothing better than their home. If they had had money, they could have updated and modernized it, but there was none. I felt as though if I said something to Adrian, I would hurt his feelings because he could not move us out, and then I would be hurting his parents' feelings too. That was probably the reason I didn't mind leaving the country with him and his friends when the opportunity materialized. I just wanted out, and I was hoping that somehow I would be able to make a difference for us, for our lives, instead of being stuck.

I had dreams, and Adrian didn't share the same opinions. He would say, "How can you even dream to have a house on your own one day? Who will pay for it? Will your parents do it? I have no money and no job that will ever be able to give you such a thing, so just stop dreaming about it. This is who we are, and we never going to get there unless we win the lottery."

The difference in age between us always stood out. He was always in control and did not always care for my opinion. He was the man, and what he decided would be how life would be. What can I say? I had my own mind, and we just did not connect. I couldn't take being crushed for no reason.

Strangely, it was hard to get used to the harmony that did exist in their house. While they were always sharing happy moments with one another, and his family was nice and fun, I had been used to growing up in a house where there was always a lot of fighting and drama. I did very much enjoy the way of life being part of a large family. Even though they didn't have much, they were always happy and positive. They taught me to see that being poor does not necessarily mean being miserable. They dealt with everyday issues much better than my family. There was so much laughter, and they were always ready for a joke. They seemed just more laid-back from how my family had lived. I think Adrian got his bad-boy reputation from the influence of his friends and wanting to show off in front of others, but I enjoyed the peace and harmony in his family very much. My mother was jealous every time I mentioned a fun story or talked about them. She felt that I enjoyed being with them more than with my own parents. The truth is that I did.

I had gotten married hastily, and we had our ups and downs. Adrian and I had a beautiful wedding. Altogether, we had about one hundred family members and friends join us. We had no money, but we managed to borrow from a friend. In Romanian weddings, it is customary that guests offer money to the bride and groom. This helps with paying the bill when the party is over, and sometimes there's a little extra left to help the newly married couple to buy themselves some furniture or food. This was how we were able to pay the entire bill after the party was finished because neither mine nor Adrian's parents were able to help at all. Fortunately, there was a bit extra left for us at the end. We had a fun wedding party; my sweet grandmother was able to come to it too. She was very proud of me. She didn't tell me she was proud, but I could see it in the way she acted in front of my aunts and uncles and cousins. But she did say, "Why so early, my dear girl? Why so early?" I had a few friends who teased me throughout the night a little. It made me a little sad. All I can say now is I hope my children have no desire of leaving home so early. I will make sure that they are happy and comfortable at home so they don't feel pressured to leave us for a long time.

I had never been the type of person to sit down and just talk about deep feelings. I guess it's because of the way my sisters and I grew up. In a way, our lives were not ours to control, at home by our parents and at school by the teachers. No one really asked us how we were feeling. No one asked if we were okay with this or that. It was a more military-like atmosphere—do this, do that, and don't ask any questions—there was never any asking why we had to do things this way. We didn't dare ask because the response would only ever be anger beating us down. Today I am learning that being more open helps a lot. I am happier and feel more at ease with myself. It took twenty-five years to get here. And I am still working on my new me, for my family and friends.

Fortunately, Adrian and I had many friends and we were socializing a lot. We would get together for movies at our home and dinner. In 1996, having a VCR and a TV was a big thing. We had a television and for a while we rented videos and movies. A group of us, maybe six to ten people, would get together and sometimes watch three or four movies in one night. Sometimes until early hours of the morning. We were all the same age, and we had the same aspirations. Other times, we would go out dancing the entire evening at a club or someone's house. In Romania, partying always meant for the entire night.

In the summer, we would go to the Black Sea for a few days. And in winter, we would go to the mountains. I never skied because it was expensive, but we just went for the scenery and to have fun. We had some very good friends who then were dating. She had an apartment in Bucharest, so sometimes the four of us would stay in Bucharest on short trips. They also had a car, so we took rides with them. Adrian and I did not even have permits to drive then. It was just for people with money or for whom it was necessary for their work. The average person didn't have a car or have a driver's permit. It was considered a luxury back then. But we got around and had a nice time with them.

I was allowed to work and found jobs easily. My first job was in a shop that sold everything from chewing gum to clothing and even electronics. I had a few other jobs as well in the two years we were in Romania before we decided to live abroad. When I met Adrian, he was working for a hotel that specialized in all kinds of health issues regarding rheumatism. Outside the city was a lake called Lacu Sarat. It contained very salty water and mud that was supposed to be amazing in treating people with arthritis and joint issues. Adrian worked on the lake. His job was to scoop the mud out and bring it to the hotel rooms for all kinds of treatments.

The lake was where I actually met him. The lake was open for tourists and civilians to visit, and I lived just outside the city, about fifteen minutes away. It was one weekend. I had gone to the lake with a few other girls, and I was sunbathing. He was there with a larger group of people. Somehow, we were introduced to each other, and we hit it off. He worked that job for the few years we lived in Romania. It was mostly a seasonal job because in the winter there were no guests at the hotel. During the winter, he would be at home. While he was working there, he also met tourists from Germany, Holland, Belgium, and France. I believe this is why his knowledge of foreign languages is so developed. We got many small presents from those tourists in exchange for small services while they were there. He was very good with people, and still is. After a while, he decided that he wanted to take a trip out of Romania to try to make extra money.

Some of Adrian's friends had success finding work in Turkey, so Adrian and his brother decided to take a bus there. They were in Turkey for about four months and did manage to find some work that gave us enough money to leave Romania. After he came back from Turkey, he decided we should leave together for Germany. After living with his family for nineteen months, we made our move in early December 1991. It was two years after the revolution, and I was now twenty years old.

Though we were allowed to leave the country, we needed a visa if we were to enter into another. There was just no way we could obtain one. Only those who had had major problems with the old communist system and whose life was in danger could obtain a visa to Germany. And you needed to be able to prove your case. We had no proof.

And so like many of our friends and other people our age, we decided to leave Romania illegally. That meant crossing the border without papers. If we were lucky enough to cross the border without getting caught, we would have a chance at a few years of secured monthly income as political refugees.

CHAPTER 2

A New Beginning

Germany, 1992

In the bitter cold of December, my husband and four of his male friends and I traveled by bus from Braila to a town in Poland that bordered on East Berlin. The trip took two nights and three days. I had never been in a bus for such a long trip before. The driver made very few stops for us to get out and walk around or use the bathroom. It was not a pleasant trip. The bus was full. There were over sixty people inside, and every single person on that bus was headed for Germany. We were all very scared about crossing over illegally, but we all had a plan. Some people would switch partners if they thought it would give them a better chance to cross safely into Germany. Most of us were between eighteen and thirty years old. We had big dreams. There was a lot of talk and great aspirations between us all. There were not many girls on that bus. That made me wonder if I was insane to be there. Was I right about making this decision? What if we never made it there? What if we were to get killed by the police in

Germany? So many questions were going through my mind. Adrian assured me that the worst that could happen to us was probably that we get arrested and spend some time in jail, but we would make it out alive. Talk about encouragement. Luckily, someone had sold us a map for two hundred German marks that helped us get about sixty miles outside Berlin.

We waited until it was dark to cross the border. As it was December, it was dark by 5:00 p.m. This gave us until the next morning to cross over about fifteen miles of fields, a relatively small mountain, and a river. The border was protected by soldiers who had dogs and guns, and if we got caught and we didn't stop, we knew they would shoot us. We heard some horrifying stories about people who had died because they kept running after being told to stop. I was so scared. I questioned myself over and over about what I was about to do. I followed my husband and our friends, but I just could not stop thinking about why I had agreed to do this. I was hoping that everything would be fine and we wouldn't die. Then I was praying that we would find work in order to pay for what we owed already for the bus trip to Poland. And in the end, I prayed that we would be safe.

Going over the mountain was not as difficult as we imagined. Although it took us about twelve hours to get through, we were mostly camouflaged by the terrain and the darkness. Then we had to go through an open field that, without trees or anything to hide behind, exposed us. To make it worse, it was windy and bitterly cold as the falling snow began turning to rain, and we were wet and frozen.

After the mountain and the field, we came to a river. The only way to cross it was to use the bridge, but doing so would expose us once again. Instead, we crossed under the bridge by holding onto the structure like children swinging from monkey bars at a playground. Fortunately, it was less than half a mile long, and we made it safely to the other side. I felt like Jane from the movie *Tarzan*. Fear and freezing-cold temperatures are an amazing combination to keep you going, and thank God it had happened at night. If I had fallen in the river below, I would have gotten wet and exposed the entire group. It didn't matter that my hands were frozen to that bar; it didn't matter that I could not feel anything anymore. All that was on my mind—

and I am sure my friends felt the same—was just to make it safely the other side and not get noticed or shot. We all crossed and started running in the open field beyond the bridge. We had to get out of the openness not to be seen by anyone. We kept running. It was so muddy, and a very cold rain dripped over our heads and bodies. I could feel the shivers going through me, but there was no time to think about that at the time. We had to get there. We weren't sure where, but we had to get somewhere safe.

At around 2:00 a.m., we made it to a small town on the border of Germany, close to Berlin. As we were congratulating one another in a park, we heard a car pulling into the parking lot. We immediately scattered quickly in all directions, hiding among small trees and very large bushes.

Four soldiers and two dogs searched for maybe ten minutes. As we were wet, the dogs couldn't smell us. We waited a while after they had left, and then with a great sigh of relief, we jumped out from behind the large plants and bushes where we had been hiding. Fortunately, the park was poorly lit, and we still weren't seen.

The whole thing was a scary experience, and to not attract attention, we decided it would be best to split up the group, so my husband and I went out on our own. We walked to the bus station and waited for the first bus of the day, due to arrive at 4:30 a.m. My husband decided to leave me at the bus station while he walked to the next one. I got on the bus and said, "*Guten morgen. Eine ticket fur Berlin.*" It worked, and after around thirty minutes, we both arrived safely in East Berlin.

We decided to split again until our next meeting point: the train to Dusseldorf. We would meet in carriage number 7, a number we picked randomly. We had no money to buy train tickets, but we knew that once we were at least one hundred kilometers from the border, the police wouldn't return and arrest us for not having tickets.

When the controller asked for our tickets, we just said, "Refugees asking for political asylum." He was used to this as Germany was full of other Romanians doing exactly the same thing as us as well as many people from Yugoslavia, Bosnia, Herzegovina, and Montenegro. He gave us each a ticket and a penalty ticket that, of course, we never paid. I felt so relieved and happy to be on that train. The train was beautiful. It even had a shower. A proper bathroom with a shower! That was where I spent twenty minutes cleaning myself after our journey through hell. It was a very luxurious train, and I could almost smell our success. We felt a tremendous relief that we had gotten in to Germany safely.

As soon as we disembarked the train in Dusseldorf, we went to the office for foreign refugees to request papers. At this time, Germany was full of foreign refugees. Once we got the papers, we were allowed to be in the country for six months at the most. We got 250 marks per month; a place to sleep, like a room in a trailer; and food stamps equaling 200 marks per month. This meant that, overall, we had 2,400 marks for the two of us for six months.

The living arrangements were so strange to us. Imagine a trailer, a very long one, made of hard metal, with about 20 rooms on each side. In the middle there were bathrooms and showers on each side. On one side was something that looked like kitchens. About 6 stove tops working on electricity and a few sinks. The place also had large industrial refrigerators aligned next to one another. The idea was that you sign a paper when you wanted to cook, and you had to wait and see if the space was going to work. If there was something that we needed to put in the refrigerator, we had to put our names on it. There were no guarantees that anything would still be there, but it was the only way we had to live. Just the way you see the refugees today on a war camp site—that's how we were living then. The difference was that I had chosen to be there. There was no war on our country at this time. We just wanted to save money and take it back home with us.

We tried to find odd jobs but had little luck as very few Germans were happy to have refugees working for them. One of my husband's friends taught us how to steal food and clothing from shops. I was always accompanied by another person. Some of the things I stole, I sold for money and immediately sent the money home to Romania. Cigarettes and alcohol sold especially well to give me extra cash. Adrian never stole anything but was good in helping me not to get caught.

When I think back on what I did, I feel ashamed. Not having the right to work was hard, and it kept us from saving. We left Romania for a reason, and that was to make a home or work and save money. We were all desperate to work—hard work, any kind of work. We just wanted to make money, but no one opened their doors to us. Immediately we felt unwanted, so we began to resent the country itself. This country had so much to offer, but at the same time there was no chance for us because we didn't have the paperwork to support ourselves. When you don't give people a chance, in my opinion, your country is ruined. That is my philosophy, having been there and lived that way. When this is a reality, you just have to look for other ways to make a dream come true. At that time, the bit of extra money ended up enabling us to return later to France. I wish we had found some work, but no one was hiring eastern Europeans. I tried even domestic stuff, like housekeeping and shop cleaning, but had no luck. As soon I opened my mouth to say where I was from, they said no thank you.

Stealing only brought in a small amount of money, and we needed more. Some people living in the same house as us had told my husband we could make more money by going to a different city and asking for asylum again. But there was a catch: you had to give a different name. We didn't know this, and we sought asylum under the same names as before. The information was kept in a computer. We did not know then that it was all taken into consideration by the German state. In the beginning, things hadn't been run this way, but the country had been getting burned by people doing this for money, and the government started keeping track of names.

Three months later we both got arrested when going to collect our monthly benefits. They had found out we had used our own names and identities in three different towns. It was fraud. We got arrested immediately as we tried to collect our monthly benefits. I felt heartbroken when I got arrested. I was so scared and so humiliated. One of my uncles got arrested a few times in Romania after stealing different grains from the fields and chickens and pigs from the farms. My relatives were all very disappointed and ashamed of him. My arrest was scary and disappointing as well. Being a woman in this situation was even worse, in my opinion. I could not believe that I had been arrested, and I was in jail in Germany.

Adrian and I were transported to different jails. I was sent to München and my husband to Koln. Mail was the only way we could communicate. We did not have access to computers or permission to use the phone. For a month or so, I had no idea where he was. As I was under twenty-one, I was considered a minor, and they gave me six months while he got eighteen months. We were not allowed to have a lawyer because we had no way to pay for one.

The detention center was a nightmare. There were hard criminals, burglars, pedophiles, and more. There were probably over two thousand other women there. All were different ages and in for different reasons. Some of them were there for murder and assault. They looked hardcore, and there was nothing that could stop them if they wanted to feel tough and important. They would beat you up if you overstepped their boundaries, even by accident. I was terrified and horribly lonely. When I got in, I spoke very little German, although by the time I got out, I was getting by, having learned it by necessity.

I was put into a cell with four beds and eventually became friends with some girls from Bulgaria and Slovenia. I cried nonstop for the first few days. I was angry because I couldn't communicate with the other girls. When I got over the shock of being in jail, I began to move beyond my fears. I mean, I was *in* now, so I had to make the best of it. We were allowed out of our cells at 6:00 a.m. and were free to walk around. At 10:00 p.m., they locked the doors again, which made me feel safe from the more serious criminals.

During the day I was constantly on guard. I had heard some horrible stories about some of the girls we were in with. Crime aside, German women can look powerful and intimidating, but these women were extra tough, with tattoos all over their bodies and punk-rock haircuts. While showering, they would give me bad looks, and my new friends and I tried to have one another's backs. Most of them received money from their families so they could buy food and were always in the kitchen cooking something. I had no money with me when I got in, and I knew there was no money on its way for me. There were other girls who were there for the same reason as me, and they didn't have much either. Perhaps because of this, we formed a special bond between us. We watched out for one another, and if one of us needed something, we helped one another to get it.

In the daytime, it was easier to endure the fact that I was in, but at night when they locked us up, it was a nightmare. Sometimes we could hear other girls screaming like animals in cages. Some of them would wait until nighttime before turning into wild animals. They would start fighting and even bringing out knives. That was when the other girls and I started to talk about our lives. Once in a while, we would hear one of the others crying herself to sleep.

Although it was terrible being inside, my happiest moments were when we went to the chapel. Once a week there was a mass held for all religions inside the chapel. The priests would come in from the churches nearby, and they were always very nice to us. The mass lasted for about an hour. During these masses was the only time in my life that I got the chance to read the entire Bible in Romanian.

We could go grocery shopping inside the prison once a week. We had something like a small grocery store, and if you had money, you could buy anything you needed. Obviously, we could not buy alcohol, but we could get ice cream and cakes. I missed not knowing more information about my husband. I had no idea if he was taken or what would happen to us. After a month, I finally received mail from him.

His prison was a lot tougher than mine. My husband's letter finally reached me, and I learned that they were only able to walk outside for one hour a day, rain or shine. He was very worried about me as no one had informed him where I had been sent. He felt guilty that I was incarcerated and that he could not help me more. It took almost two weeks for letters to travel between us.

I was too embarrassed to write to my parents. What was I going to say? "I am in a jail in Germany, be proud of me"? I was so ashamed and scared.

Around the same time as Adrian's letter, a month after I was imprisoned, I got a letter stating that I would be going to court. For the next month, that was all I could think and talk about. I was terrified. I barely spoke German and had no idea what to expect.

Some girls inside said they had been there for two years for the same crime. Anything was possible, and not knowing what was going to happen made it even more difficult to bear. I was very young when it all happened, thank God, so I was not destroyed by depression. I was scared and emotionally disturbed, but I had the strength to keep myself together and get out. My emotions were running wild, but I was just taking one day at a time. There was not much I could have done to change my fate. All I was able to do was to behave and wait to hear more news.

The day of my court date, I was put into a special transporter bus with small rooms and I was handcuffed to the seat. My hands were tied to the chair and feet tied to the floor. Thank God I was young when all this happened. I don't know if I could handle it now.

When I walked into the courtroom, I was overjoyed to see my husband. We sat next to each other but were not allowed to look at or touch each other. I hadn't seen him for two months, and now I was not even allowed to give him a hug. It seemed like forever until our sentences were pronounced. My husband got one more year, but I was freed. I couldn't believe it. Because I was not yet twenty-one, they held him responsible for "forcing" me to commit the crime of asking for political asylum under a false name. I was happy to be out, but still I was scared.

I walked out a free person. But now I had a different dilemma: where do I go? I had no money and no friends. I had nothing and knew nothing about the city I was in. I had maybe only twenty German marks in my pocket. I was scared for the future.

And then I remembered some girls in prison talking about a place where young people go, often students, to crash when they have no money. I went there, and they received me well, asking only a few questions about my situation. It was a nonprofit organization that was able to offer me a bed in a large dormitory that I shared with more than six people. There was a communal bathroom to share with everyone. We had all three meals free as well, and I am sure that if my German language was better, I probably could have been able to make some friends or even find some work. The maximum time we were allowed to stay in the dorms for the first time was a week. I kept very quiet and felt relieved that I had a place to sleep and something to eat until I figured out my next move. I went for long walks and explored the city by foot. I was very lonely and lost. Of course, I felt so happy to be free from jail, and I counted my blessings that I was released after not too much time inside. As well as that, I was healthy and all in one piece. When I was younger, I never overthought many of my decisions. I knew I had to make decisions, and I stuck with them. There were no alternatives. In a way, this worked better for me because I wasn't overcome by conflicting emotions. Overthinking it would have brought many more issues. To do or not to do? I managed to keep my sanity through all those events the best I could. I enjoyed the place where I was now and wished I could have stay there longer. In many ways, it was like a hostel with lots of young people around. There was a catch, though. The maximum stay there was one full week. There were some other people from eastern Europe just like me who were in the same situation. There were also lots of young German kids. They were accommodating people as young as eighteen. Some of those young Germans were really rebellious. Many of them had tattoos all over their bodies, rings through their noses, unusual haircuts, and really strange choices of clothing. Perhaps I was quick to judge, but their appearances and styles were so different from the kids back home. At night the lights went off at 11:00 p.m., but they continued to play music. Their music choices were horrencous too.

I only ended up staying there for a day. After a few hours, I began chatting with another young woman there, and I told her a little about my story. She advised me to go back to the place I was living before I got arrested. It was not too far away, just a train ride, so I went. I went in, and as soon as I opened my mouth and told them my name, I found myself in big trouble once again. I had made a huge mistake.

I hadn't been in my room for more than thirty minutes when the police were at my door with an arrest warrant for me and one for my husband, issued a few months back from a town near München. We had applied there for a political refuge petition under a fake name.

For the second time, I got arrested and went immediately back to jail. Stupid. If I hadn't gone back to that place, this might not have happened. Still, since I knew what to expect, I was not as frightened as the first time. With that said, I was very upset about going through it all over again. I knew that somehow I needed to tell Adrian that I was in prison again, this time in a different city and place. He found out about it a week later and was shocked that I was in again. It was hard communicating through just letters because so much time passes between receiving the next piece; today's news is old in a week's time.

They sent me to a women's prison in Koln. Unlike in the first prison, we had to stay in our cell for twenty-three hours a day with just one hour per day for a walk outside. We were allowed a thirty-minute shower once a week on Fridays, and that was it.

When I arrived, they left me alone in a small cell. I was terrified. I did not know what they intended to do with me. Normally, being alone in a cell is for isolation or because you're being punished for being a bad inmate. Knowing that from my first experience, after a few hours, I exploded, sobbing, shouting, and banging on the door.

Finally, they felt sorry for me, or maybe they were just annoyed, and moved me into a room with three other girls. I was relieved. Even though the others were from Lithuania and Slovenia and spoke neither German nor Romanian, I was so grateful to share space with another human. At least I had company. A smile or even just eye contact can mean a lot in these situations. Eventually we figured out ways to communicate with one another. They all seemed like nice girls, the same age as me, and in for the same reason. We played lots of card games and talked about our lives in a mix of languages. When you have so much time to yourself, you somehow get creative. I had even kept a journal while I was there. Unfortunately, I don't have it anymore, but writing my thoughts down helped me get through each day. Again, I had no idea how long I was in for or what they were going to do with me. Was I going to stand up again in front of a judge? Would I ever see Adrian again? Would they keep me in longer now because it was my second time? Would they find out about the rest of the places I gave more fake names to receive more money? Not knowing was terrifying.

There was a small window I could look out of, and I noticed that every day at 8:00 a.m., some girls would walk into a building next door, emerging again at 4:00 p.m. I asked one of the guards where they were going, and she told me they were going to work. They were tasked with assembling broken jewelry and repacking it. When I asked how I could work too, she informed me that only girls who with exemplary behavior get in. From that moment on, I was always on my best behavior until eventually I got in. Not that I ever misbehaved, but I made sure that every time a guard opened the small gate to give us food, I had something nice to say and a big smile on my face. And it worked.

I loved being busy. I was making around ten marks a day and could spend the money in the prison shop. I bought extra cookies, juices, toiletries. It was as close as I had to heaven. I even managed to send twenty marks to my husband along with some stamps. I even began to communicate with my sisters and parents through mail. We were asked to look through small jewelry items that came back from shops either broken or just mismatching. We had to change labels on them and reassemble the pieces. It was actually very nice while we were doing it, and it really helped calm down our nerves. Also from 8:00 a.m. to 4:00 p.m., I was busy working, so I was out of the cell. I even had the right to have a shower every day after we finished work. That was a real bonus. By the time we got done with work, it would be dinner time and at 9:00 p.m., lights were out, and it was time for bed. Time was passing more quickly, and it wasn't as terrible as before.

One morning, after around three months of being imprisoned, I woke up to a loud banging on my door. It was earlier than usual, so I immediately panicked. The man on guard entered the room and told me to start packing. He said I was going to leave that day. When I asked where I was going, they said, "To Zurich, and from there to Romania." I was trembling with happiness at the thought of getting out and going home. I asked the guard to tell me if Adrian was also leaving, but he said he did not know that information. I didn't think he would have known, but it was worth a shot to ask.

I was handcuffed and put into a jail bus to get to the airport, and from there I was put on a jail plane, where I remained handcuffed through the entire flight. They really made me feel like a criminal all the way. There were no smiles, no snacks, no talking. Flying handcuffed to a bar and not even allowed to stand for a second except a quick bathroom break was really something I never want experience again in my life. The entire plane was full of Romanians coming from different prisons from Germany for different crimes. No one was interested in making small talk, and there was no music or TV on the flight either. I landed in Bucharest with no one knowing that I was there. I had no money with me. But I was home.

I made a collect call to my mother-in-law, who had a phone at her house. My parents would not have a phone for many years yet. I had to tell someone I was home. No one had heard from me in weeks. They were very happy and surprised that I had finally made it home. Or almost home. Bucharest is a three-hour trip by car from my city. My mother-in-law told me not to worry; she had a cousin who lives in Bucharest. "Just stay where you are and don't move," she said. Not like I had anywhere else to go to. She called her cousin, and just about an hour or so later, they came to get me. They were very nice, but for someone who had never met me, they grilled me with questions. But I didn't mind as finally I could speak my own language and was free again to do as I pleased. I slept at their home overnight, and they lent me the money to take a train back to Braila the next day.

Being home was difficult. While I was excited to be home and out of prison, I felt guilty for my behavior. And it was awkward living with my in-laws without my husband, even though they were nice and treated me well. I went to see my parents almost daily, and I visited my grandma as often as I could. I tried keeping busy by hanging out with my sisters and friends, but it was difficult to do much not knowing when Adrian would be liberated from Germany. Every few weeks, I would receive a letter from him telling me that he still had no court date or any idea when he will be able to come home.

France, 1993

It was three months later when Adrian came back to Romania. Finally, we were together again and decided to give going abroad another shot. This time in France. In no time, we started planning how we could leave again. We had managed to save some money before we both had been arrested in Germany, and we decided to buy a real ticket to Paris. Buying a trip through a travel agent meant that we would not have to travel illegally like we had done before in Germany. After almost a month of waiting to hear if we would get our visas to France, we were finally approved. It took all the savings we had, but this time we left in a plane. It was the first plane ride we had spent with each other. Before now, we had been alone and chained to our seats on our plane rides. We were very excited about the future again.

We arrived in Paris in September along with some of our friends. It was so beautiful, just as we dreamed it would be. Lights, beautiful buildings, huge avenues, trees along the streets. The trip that we booked included a stay in a hotel for five nights. The five nights went by very quickly. In this time, we had already started making plans about what we would do next. We both spoke French. Adrian was actually very good. He had always been good with foreign languages, and as for me, I was definitely improving and being understood without too much stress. Already I felt better about being in France. We visited the Eiffel Tower the night we arrived. The friends who came along with us were all men, but we all got along very well. It was fun to have friends with us because we all helped one another out. The Eiffel Tower was amazing. That night we walked there from our hotel. We had no money for a taxi. We took a map from the hotel, and we had a beautiful stroll through the city of lights. Even to this day, I clearly remember the fun we had that night. For all of us, it was the first time we had been to Paris, so everything felt amazing and the energy and excitement glowed around us. I had always loved the sound of the French language. I could not believe that I was finally there.

Once we got to the tower, we walked up to the top. We had no money to pay for the elevators, but we didn't mind. Just like a dream come true. The view from the top was spectacular. I remember walking the streets of Paris and just jumping up and down with excitement. Paris gave me a special buzz. Lots of people talk that way about New York, but to me Paris is breathtakingly beautiful. There was so much culture, amazing architecture, and the Seine that splits the city with boats that cruise the river. It just had charm. I fell in love with Paris. Unfortunately, there were not many opportunities for us in Paris, so eventually we decided to go further down south. Adrian had friends living in the south of France, far from Paris, so we decided to visit them.

As we had no money for the train or bus, we hitchhiked. Following a map, we made our way to the entrance of a large highway that traveled south. After an hour of standing on the roadside with our thumbs out, still no one stopped to pick us up. There were many police officers around, and after Germany, this made us nervous.

We decided he should wait close by, but out of sight, I tried to hitch a ride alone. After twenty minutes or so, an older French gentleman pulled over. He asked where I was going, and all I said was, "*Sud*" (South). He told me to hop in. I told him I was with my husband, and Adrian appeared at my side. He looked us over and invited us to hop in. Adrian sat in the front, and I in the back seat.

My French was poor, but Adrian was fluent, and they quickly started chatting. His name was Guy. He told us that he was going to Valence, toward the south, a town just outside Lyon and a six-hour drive from Paris. As we had nothing to lose, we said we would be happy to go to Valence.

After driving for a few hours, Guy stopped for coffee and asked us to join him. We only had the equivalent of a hundred dollars total with us for our whole stay in France and felt embarrassed about what to order. But Guy was an angel sent from heaven. He treated us to a great lunch, and we began to talk about our plans for the future.

We learned that Guy was the director of a large chemical manufacturing company in Valence. He had many connections in town, and he offered to try to help get us jobs and a house. Guy became our guardian angel for our entire stay in France. We had hit the jackpot.

We arrived in Valence at around five in the evening. As we had no place to stay, Guy took us to a church where he was close friends with the priest. We explained our story, and the priest sent us to a place in town for students with low income. As I was just twenty-two, they let us stay and gave us a studio with a small bathroom. The place itself was an establishment strictly for helping young people, so our age was very important.

We said good night to Guy and exchanged phone numbers, agreeing to meet the next day. The next morning, he took us shopping. We got the essentials we needed for our little studio and to fill the fridge and freezer with food. Guy paid for everything.

The following day he sent us to a charity called Sans-Abri, a place that means "without a home." They were helping people in need of jobs, and if people were sick or in desperate need of medical help, they would offer advice and point them in the right direction. They sold newspapers for two franks that they suggested we resell for five francs. That was actually how they managed people in our situation. There were lots of French locals, people who were doing the same thing. It was just like in the US when there are homeless people on the streets; this was an opportunity for us to do something and make some money. Instead of forcing us to beg out in the street or to steal, we had a chance to earn some money. The newspapers could be sold everywhere. I mean, if you were French, this would have been legal, but for us, as outsiders? We had to be very careful with the police. For two years, this was what we did. It enabled us to live and survive in France.

To get around the illegality of the job, we would go to the main intersections with traffic lights. I would walk between cars carrying around twenty papers at a time. I had to be very fast as the light would change quickly and I could not block the traffic. Adrian stayed just behind the light, checking for the police.

All in all, our risky enterprise gave us the money we needed to pay rent for five hundred francs per month and three hundred francs to buy food and clothes and to send money home. Sometimes we also found odd jobs, like cutting pieces of firewood, cleaning houses, and washing windows.

In spite of all this hard work, we loved France and we enjoyed ourselves. For almost two months we decided to leave Valence and went to visit a Romanian friend, who was a few hours away. He told us that he was staying in a house that belonged to a French man who needed some construction done on his home. We decided to take the job. We ended up doing all kinds of small jobs for him. He was an older gentleman and turned out to be really nice. He let us stay in his house without charging us. In exchange for our work, he gave us some cash and food for the entirety of our stay. At some point during our time there, he had to leave on a short trip, so he let us stay in the house and watch over his cats. It was the three of us while he was gone. Adrian and I and this friend were there with for almost two months. We got to meet the neighbors and get acclimated to the entire town. It was a very small suburban town with a lot of charm.

We managed to survive in his absence with only one small incident. He had a beautiful collection of wines. He told us that we could not open any as they were very precious to him. I'm still not sure if Adrian had the idea or my other Romanian friend, but they decided to open some of his wine and replace the wine inside with cheaper wine. Really, I don't know why we did that. Maybe because he had such a large number of bottles, they thought he would never notice. Unfortunately, when he came home, he noticed right away, and he threw us out of his home. I was very embarrassed, especially because he had been so nice to us. We had to leave town without the last money he owed us for the work we had done. He kept that as payment for the wine, he said. Sometimes we made really stupid mistakes. We went back to Valence to sell newspapers again.

One weekend, Guy proposed that we join him on a trip to Marseille. He had some business to attend to, and we took his offer to go along. By now, we knew one another very well, and we had a great time traveling together. We came back to Guy the next day and went to Marseille. It was a really beautiful city. We went to a fish market and saw the old town. We even went on a small boat trip. We were very happy tourists.

Our marriage had not been easy, but in France our relationship started to feel right. Especially without the encumbrance of having his parents lording over us and watching every move.

We had also met other Romanian friends from our city while we lived in Valence. All in all, there were about ten of us—all guys except for me. They treated me with respect because I was working hard, harder than their wives or girlfriends they had left back home in Romania. Many times, they slept over at our house because they had run out of money to pay rent or they just wanted to crash somewhere for a while. Adrian loved hosting, and so did I.

During this time, our friendship with Guy, who would invite us to his house to meet his family for dinner, got even better. At one point, he invited two other couples to meet us, and they offered us potential small jobs for the future.

We were thrilled with the way our life was starting to take shape. Everyone was treating us as equals. It felt wonderful to be so far from home and finally making a life for ourselves. We went out with other couples. In the winter, we went ice-skating. Unfortunately, I fell and broke my arm, which required surgery. We called Guy, who took us to a good hospital. They operated on me immediately with no charge. Apparently, it was done as a favor to Guy, who held a high position in town. Again, we counted our blessings.

I had to wear a cast for three months, and this made it hard to go back to selling newspapers. But we had no choice. Although there was little snow in Valence during the winter, it was very windy, and the air was a bitter dry cold. In spite of it all, I did what I had to do for us to survive.

By selling newspapers, I had the opportunity to meet lots of people. Some were nasty and treated me disrespectfully, asking if I could meet them for drinks and dates. But some offered me small jobs, like housecleaning or cutting wood. My familiarity with the customers grew every day. Overall, it was tolerable, and we made it through the winter. It also helped that we were meeting up with Guy and his family and friends almost every other week.

Romania, 1995

After almost two years of this life, we decided to return to Romania. It was impossible to legally stay in France without papers, and it became too stressful to always watch out for police. Our chances of becoming legal were limited. And of course, we did not want to end up in jail again. We had saved enough money to buy an apartment in Romania and hopefully live happily ever after.

We had an overall good experience in France. We meet some extraordinary people, and we enjoyed ourselves as well as working and saving money. My French got so much better, and I really enjoyed my time there. We unfortunately had lost touch with our dear friend Guy. I also have not been back to Valence since then, but I promised myself that one day I will return with my family.

We returned home in January, and soon after, we bought a small two-bedroom apartment with the money we had managed to save in France, which came to the equivalent of roughly five thousand dollars today. Although it was small, we loved it. We were very close to my parents this time, and we furnished it to make it feel like a home. We got to meet the neighbors, we had family over, and we entertained our friends. We were trying to get used to living in our own home. Because we were both used to being outside, we got bored easily. How much socializing could we do with family and friends? It became like a chore after a while. We both started getting bored of being at home, and our minds were working on what was next for us.

We knew we had to find work. As neither one of us had any college education, there was not much we could do except sales or waitressing and bartending. I found a job for a couple of months in a boutique that sold clothes and developed pictures at the same time. Adrian felt too smart to do menial work, so I was the only one who worked. A pattern emerged—I worked while Adrian didn't. By July, both of us were itching to leave Romania again. We wanted our lives to be exciting once more.

We thought of going back to France. But then we ran into an old friend of Adrian's, Fluturas, who lived in New York and was vacationing in Braila. His parents had a home on the same street as

Adrian's parents, my mother-in-law told us one day. When Adrian heard he was back visiting his mother, he called him right away. We went to meet him that same afternoon. He was a very nice-looking man in his midthirties, Americanized a little. His accent had changed. He raved about his life as an American citizen, where he worked as a doorman in a fancy building in Manhattan. He talked to us about his salary and his lifestyle in the US. We were listening to him, and both of us were mesmerized by his stories. We asked probably a thousand questions about America. His favorite musician was Bruce Springsteen. It all sounded surreal at the time, and the more I listened, the more I felt excited about going to the US.

    It was hard, almost impossible, to obtain a visa to the US. Fluturas promised he would help us to get ours. We went home that evening, and we started to hate our small life at home. It just felt like a tiny village, and now we both had America in our dreams. The next few days we worked on everything we needed to show to the US embassy. They had lots of papers and demands. Then when we had it all, we begged Fluturas to come with us to the embassy to apply for the visa. I remember the huge line outside and those very tall gates. There were over hundred people in line, all for the same reason as us. We were both so stressed, and we kept watching how some people would come out of those gates crying with happiness and some would leave crying in desperation because they had been refused. After we got inside through the big gates, we became even more anxious. There was a huge room with lots of desks and windows, and we were given a number. When our number appeared on the screen, we had to stand up and go to the right window. We were watching the faces of other people to see how they were doing. There were such direct questions and so many that it was overwhelming. Some people were really crying and explaining their entire life stories to the interviewing officers. Some of them really had no heart. They were such well-trained people and seemed so stiff. Miraculously, when it was our turn, we obtained a ten-year visa. Even today I can't believe how lucky we had gotten. That was the ticket to freedom we had hoped and fought for years before. We walked outside the embassy and started screaming and jumping up and down with joy. We called our family to share the good news with them. We were ecstatic. We drove back to our city and started packing right away. We booked our tickets for New York on that same day as well. It was beyond amazing that everything had changed for us in one day. A new future, new hopes, new dreams. We were on such a high. We started to go see our friends and say our goodbyes. My parents thought I was crazy to leave again. They were pleased to have me living in the same neighborhood as them. They could see me every day and stop by on weekends for a meal together.

At the time, we had taken in a cat from the street. We called him Marcello, and we fell in love with him. We found him when he was only a few days old, left out on the street just after we came back from France. At this time, he was about six months old. I just could not imagine leaving him behind. He was our baby, so we made our decision to take him with us. In Romania at the time, people would not keep their pets inside the house. Dogs and cats were mostly outside animals. So for us to even worry about our cat was really an unusual issue. With this decided, we started calling the airline to find out what we needed to do in order for him to come with us. We got his vaccines done and his passport made, and we also got a cage for him for the plane. It was all happening. Lots of our friends and family laughed at us for wanting to take our kitten with us. But when the day arrived, we hadn't changed our minds. On the plane, he was an angel. We spent the hours chatting and feeling excited to arrive in New York. Our dear friend Fluturas waited for us at airport. He was shocked when he saw us walk through the doors with the cat. He had a huge bouquet of roses for me. I still have a picture that he took of me with the cat in one hand and flowers in the other. I had a huge smile on my face that said, "America, here we are!"

New York, 1995

We arrived at John F. Kennedy Airport in New York in September 1995. What a beautiful day! A new beginning in what I considered to be the best country in the world. Everyone in Eastern Europe shared this view of America too. Adrian and I both felt like we knew so much about New York already. We had seen photos of Manhattan in the movies, and Times Square and the Brooklyn Bridge, the Statue of Liberty, and the Empire State Building. But nothing prepared us for how different real life was.

We got into Fluturas's large suburban car and drove to his place in Astoria, Queens, a two-bedroom apartment that he was living in alone. I was mesmerized from the car ride alone. It was a nice apartment that even had a doorman, so we were already impressed. We changed and left the cat, and off we went to explore the city. Fluturas drove us to Manhattan. It was nighttime, and the lights that lit up the sky as we crossed the bridge from Queens to Manhattan were breathtaking. I pinched myself to make sure I wasn't dreaming.

We walked the city streets for a couple of hours, and it felt like we were walking on clouds. We had dinner in the McDonald's in Times Square. Everything was so huge that we had to take lots of photos and just read every poster that was lit up on Times Square. We stopped and watched people going by, everyone minding their own business. I really wanted to stop everyone and tell them that we had made it and we were from far away. We went to bed in the early hours of the morning and dreamed all about this amazing new place.

When we got up the next day, we started thinking about where we should start. We were worried, as well as nervous, about another beginning. We had sold our apartment in Romania for around three thousand dollars so we had some cash in our pockets, but we needed to make more. Our friend gave us some ideas about where to start looking for a job. Honestly I spoke no English at all. My French, Romanian, and German did not help at all, so I was scared about how I was going to make it. We had some money we had brought with us from home, so we started by looking for a place to rent. Because we didn't want to pay a fee to an agency, we started by looking for ads in the paper to rent directly from the owner.

In a few days, we rented a two-bedroom apartment in Queens with a little garden. It was unfurnished. Now we needed furniture, and there was no money for that. We found out that every evening at 10:00 p.m. people discarded their old or unwanted furniture on the street, and we found enough to make ourselves a home. We managed to furnish the entire place with items from the streets, including the bed we slept on. We did buy sheets and pillows from some cheap Chinese stores we found. Looking back now, I find it crazy how we were able to manage, but at the time I felt very lucky to have what we had. It's true that when you are in a tough situation, you put up with whatever is necessary to pull through. We hit the streets the next day looking for work. We left the house together in the morning, and we started to walk the streets. I knew I spoke no English, so I was looking for something to do where I wouldn't be required to talk. I just wasn't sure what. Maybe cleaning homes or shops. We went to a large dry cleaning, and Adrian asked the owners if I could work there. They needed girls to iron, mostly shirts. At the time, the lowest salary per hour was $5.00. They would give me $3.50 per hour because I had no papers. I was desperate to work, but I had to refuse that offer. They also wanted me to work through weekends and holidays. The majority of the workers were Chinese. I kept going from restaurant to restaurant. Even some shops, but because I spoke barely any English, I got refused right away. After a week, I landed a job as a waitress in a Greek café, Billiard. The owner was Greek and seemed to like me. I think he recognized an opportunity in me to save himself some money and to work me as much as he needed me. In general, he treated me nicely when I worked there, but the staff were not as welcoming. I felt lucky just to have a job in under a week of living in New York. Adrian had not found anything yet. We were complete opposites.

    I was terrified because of my lack of English, but I managed. They served mainly to kids and had no food, only a few desserts on the menu, along with beers and sodas, coffees, frappes, and teas. I only had to learn what those were to take an order. Easier said than done in real life. And I did get my fair share of reality once I started.

    I was bullied as most of the customers were between sixteen and twenty-five. One time someone asked me for a few napkins and straws. As always, I went straight to ask the bartender for their request. That was the system: I took the order from the customers, and then I go to the bar to request the drinks to be made. I couldn't understand the words for *napkins* or *straws* in English because of how limited my English was at the time. On a different occasion, someone asked me for Coke. Again, I went to the bartender to request it, and because by now they were annoyed with me, they told me to go back to the customer and tell them no drugs today. Everyone laughed, and I felt humiliated. I went through a few other similar episodes until my English began to improve. The job was also hard because my shift was from 10:00 p.m. to 4:00 a.m., and that messed up my circadian rhythm and ruined my sleep.

Adrian and I had been married for five years, and he had not been able to hold a job for more than just a few weeks each time. I was getting more and more disillusioned with the marriage. Wasn't the husband supposed to be the one to ensure the family's survival? The men should carry their weight financially, and the women can come in handy with other things. Today, equal rights between men and women and the role of each in a family has changed, but I was born into this way thinking. Of course, it could have been circumstantial, but I still felt uneasy.

Since I felt I couldn't rely on him, I decided to leave the job at the Greek café in early December and move up to look for work in Manhattan. By now my English had improved enough that I had more choices when it came to work. Not only that, but I was tired of the night shift.

I found a coat check job at Café Ciello, an Italian restaurant on Eighth Avenue, that served great food. I worked lunch and dinner every day from 11:00 a.m. to 11:00 p.m. or 12:00 a.m. I had a window between 3:00 and 5:00 p.m. when I was free and on my own. As it didn't give me enough time to go home, I would go for a walk around the city, or if it was too cold, I would nap in the back of the restaurant by laying across a few chairs. The girls who were working in the restaurant would always hang around together on their break or they would be out running errands. Because my knowledge of English was still limited, or perhaps because my clothing style was different to theirs, I was never close to any of them. There was always a respect between us, but things remained very formal. One of the girls approached me one day while working and told me that

I smelled of sweat and I should use a deodorant more often. She even went as far as suggesting that maybe I need to wash my clothes with a specific detergent. I am sure I probably smelled of body odor because I was there from 10:30 a.m. until midnight every single day. There were other ways they could have approached me to tell me that without any embarrassment, but maybe it was their intention to make me feel bad. After a short while and after the remark I got from them, I decided to bring a change of clothes for dinner every day and wash in the restaurant bathroom. This made me feel humiliated, and I didn't want to be embarrassed at work again. When the girls began to notice some customers had been taking an interest in me, they became even more distant.

Joe, the owner of the restaurant, was a nice man, in his late fifties, and divorced. He always had a smile on his face for customers, though at times he blew his top with the staff. With me, he was always kind and chatty, and through conversation with him and the customers, I began to learn English. Customers treated me with respect and seemed interested in conversing in spite of my broken English.

The restaurant attracted many nice people as well as many celebrities, such as musicians and show people. It was a great job for me. All I had to do was look pretty and smile. By spring, my English was better but not good enough to become a waitress, and in April, I had to leave the job. With warmer weather, people no longer wore coats out to eat.

I did not feel afraid to go out and look for a job this time as I had learned so much there and felt myself growing as a person. Joe assured me I could return in the fall if I wanted to. Unfortunately, he never allowed me to work as a waitress or bartender because my accent was too strong, and he thought the customers wouldn't understand me. In no time, I found a waitressing job at an Italian restaurant on the Upper West side. And it was lucky that I did as Adrian was still out of work. This put a great strain on our marriage. After six years of being the one to keep the family going, I had had enough. Nor did I feel I could handle his concerns about me sending my family money anymore.

When I asked Adrian for a divorce, he refused and said he would stay in our apartment and I would have to find another place. He said this because he was sure I would never have the courage to move out or have the money for a divorce lawyer. But he was wrong.

I got myself a small basement apartment and filed for divorced. He was in shock. He was so upset and wild the night before I left. For months I got phone calls at different hours, day and night. He was sharing our place with my sister and her husband now, and she told me he was drinking himself to death. Many times, he would look through the windows of my basement trying to see if I was with someone else. Some of our male friends would visit me, and on their way out, he would surprise them at the door and tell them that they should never come to see me again. He was crazy jealous. He was a desperate man, and I know he did all those because he was hurt by my decision to leave him. I just wasn't in love anymore, and we had become more like roommates than a couple.

As for me, I felt sad to have to go through a divorce, but I finally felt freedom. For the first time, I could do what I wanted without having to answer to anyone—not my parents or his family. He had always consulted his mother for advice on what to do, and I was glad to be free of that.

I didn't hate him. All in all, I think Adrian was a great guy as a friend. Smart and funny, he was great company to hang out with. When I met him at only seventeen, he impressed me as a strong, intelligent, and popular guy with lots of friends. But after those six years together, I outgrew him.

After so much travel, meeting many new and interesting people, and having so many life-changing experiences, I wanted more from life than he did, and unlike him, I strived to work for it. Our views over the future had changed. We no longer shared the same dream, and I was tired of feeling guilty for thinking differently. On top of that, carrying the work burden for so long made me feel as if he was piggybacking on me for a free ride, whether this was true or not. And so I left, though I will always be grateful to him for having the vision for us to leave Romania.

Though I had a ten-year visa in the US, the visa was only good if I didn't stay more than six months at a time. I had now been in the country for one whole year, and during that time, both Adrian and I had returned to Romania twice. We stayed for two to three weeks and then returned to the US.

After the divorce, I returned to Romania alone. It was hard for me as being divorced was shameful and I felt embarrassed. At least, the first time I went back I was embarrassed. My in-laws were upset with me, but even though I knew this, I still went to their house to see everyone. His brothers and sisters were happy to see me. I am sure they all thought we might still get back together after my return to the US. My parents were unhappy with my situation and asked me to stay in Romania. I told them, "Not in a million years," because I had finally really started my life. My sister Lili was there, and I had made some friends, mostly Romanians, but also some Americans, and the US felt like home.

I returned to New York in early September. Though I was happy to be divorced, I missed having a family, and I felt a bit lonely between just working and spending time in in my basement apartment. When I moved out from my place with Adrian, I took my cat, Marcello, with me. He spent a lot of time alone inside the house. I took him for a walk each day before I went to work and again after I came back. I lived close to Astoria Park, so it was very easy and enjoyable. Few of my Romanian friends hung out with me anymore because they were married, and their husbands forbade them from speaking with me, a "liberal" divorced woman. One of our dear friends, Ana, had divorced her husband too, and this shocked our friends. They started wondering who would be next.

It hurt to be ostracized from them, but Ana and I became closer because of it. We got ourselves a basement apartment a little larger than the one I had and moved in together. Now when I came home from work, I wasn't alone as we had each other. That was the beginning of a long and beautiful friendship, and we are good friends even today.

My sister Lili was still living with her husband and my ex, but a few months later she ended up divorcing her Romanian husband too, and we were really the talk of our small Romanian community. I no longer cared. She ended up having an affair with someone she met while she was working as a waitress. It took us all by surprise, but she explained that she and her husband had fallen out of love for quite some time already. I was not very proud of her for doing that, but it was not up to me to make her choices.

Our poor parents were really not happy with us. We left Romania for a better life, and so far, for my parents, life in US had done nothing but destroy us. I can see now how in the eyes of a parent this was terrible. At least they still had one daughter left home and they were keeping her on an even shorter leash than they had kept us. Nicole was suffocating. She was underage, so she could not yet join us. She was not allowed to have a passport until she turned eighteen, and there was one more year to go before that. In addition, she still had to finish high school.

Stanley

In late October 1997, I missed the friends I had eventually made at Café Cielo and went back to work there part-time. I always loved the atmosphere there even though some of the waitresses still did not like me very much. Joe was still the owner there, and the customers were regulars who came back over and over again. Lots of them knew one another, so they would also chat between themselves. They were very well-mannered gentlemen who always spoke with me. As a matter of fact, this was how I broke down my English problem, just by chatting with anyone who was at the bar. That was where I had to stay to wait for the customers to walk inside. Then I would ask for their coats or umbrellas. Sometimes, even if they did not check anything, I was still tipped. It was nice to see them and always felt like we were good friends. I met many interesting people there. The café was located on Eighth Avenue and Fifty-Second Street. The crowd we attracted at lunch was almost always the same, all business people from the insurance company next door. Many actors and actresses from Broadway shows on the next avenue came over too. We met famous musicians. Paul Schafer, who worked—and still works—on the *David Letterman Show*, was there every day at lunch. He was a very nice, interesting man, always smiling and very calm. Every day he would order the same pasta dish. He hugged me each time he saw me, asked me what was new, and would listen and chat.

I loved seeing the customers come back every day at lunch. Joe was always wonderful at making them feel at home. He asked them questions about work, family, their kids. He was a great guy, and I guess that's why they came back year after year. In the evening, the crowd was a bit different. It was mostly tourists or people in town to see a Broadway show. The food was excellent, and there was a great atmosphere too. Joe was always there. He worked very hard. It was a lot of work as I was still working part-time waitressing at the other restaurant, but I was making good money. It felt great to be free and making a future for myself.

But that wasn't the best of it. At the café, I met Stanley, a divorced man, twenty-five years older than me, and almost my father's age. I knew him from the previous winter when I worked at Cielo. At the time he had a girlfriend. She was very beautiful, a model, blond, tall, and skinny. Exactly how he liked his women. She had it all. But I noticed that every time they came in for dinner, and that was at least three times a week, she always looked miserable. At this time, a few months had passed, and they were not together anymore. He and I got to talking. She had moved back to her hometown, Sacramento, California. He asked me out to celebrate his forty-ninth birthday. The same age as my father. But he was cool. There was something about him that I was attracted to.

He had a unique style that I found I was attracted to right away. He wore long leather cowboy boots over tight jeans. His body was slim, so this choice suited him. In the six years we spent together, I probably saw him wear a suit only twice. He wore his shirts tucked in to big belts and always finished the look with a baseball hat. His closet was filled with boots and jeans. In the winter, he would wear the same outfits but with a leather jacket on top, strong colors, but never black. His outfits matched his character. Stanley was funny, but always very polite, and generous with his words and his money most of the time. He worked hard and had a good business ethic. He could tell if someone was good or bad just by having a quick conversation with them.

That night, Stanley made plans for us to get together for dinner and a show for his birthday. He had sent me out shopping to Bloomingdale's, where a sales assistant met me and helped me choose an outfit for the evening. Then I had a makeup and a hair appointment. I was a very busy lady and super excited for the evening. He sent me out with his chauffer from place to place. After I was done, he let me change into my new outfit in his place in Manhattan. We went out with another couple who were very close with him. He definitely knew how to make a woman fall in love with him from the first date. It was an amazing night. I also slept at his place in Manhattan that night, but I refused to make love with him on the first night. I told him that I didn't know him well enough, and the next morning I went back to work and sent him a nice text message thanking him for a special evening.

After that first day, we met weekly for a while, and I spent more and more time with him, almost to the point I had started living at his place. It happened so fast. He had three children: a twelve-year-old daughter; a fourteen-year-old son, who was mentally disabled; and a sixteen-year-old son. The children lived with his ex-wife in Brooklyn and spent time with Stanley on most weekends and some holidays. Nevertheless, Stanley had a lot on his plate caring for them. His divorce with his ex-wife was terrible, and for the six years he and I were together, they were in a constant battle over his income. She believed he wasn't giving her enough child support, and it made him upset. He was a very kind and gentle person who loved his children very much. And he had health issues, like headaches, backaches, and knee problems. At the time it didn't bother me, but I should have been more concerned. Outside our relationship, he had two close friends, but he was still very lonely. He often visited his mom in Brooklyn just to make sure she was keeping herself busy and active. Looking back, I knew he was capable of giving me more love and attention, but there were so many other factors in his life. It made me very sad.

NOT TOO LONG AGO

I didn't mind the age difference between us because we had a lot of fun together. Another thing that attracted me to him was the love we both shared for old, classic movies. We would spend some weekends in upstate New York just cooking and listening to Frank Sinatra or the Eagles, Tony Bennett, and Neil Diamond and binge-watching classic movies. Other times, we would go to Broadway shows, and as often as five days a week, we would eat in very nice restaurants. Occasionally he took me shopping and treated me with nice clothes that I never could have afforded on my own. Often, we both went to visit his wonderful mother. She was Italian and a very special lady who loved life and fashion as much as I did. We would cook, eat, drink, and take long walks together.

All in all, I loved our relationship, though, truthfully, it could be turbulent. While a sweet and respectful man for the majority of our time together, Stanley could be demanding, domineering, obsessive, and jealous, and occasionally he tried to control me. Especially when it came to my time and my sisters.

By the time I had started dating Stanley, my younger sister, Nicole, had turned eighteen and had gotten her visa. She had come to the US, and the three of us—Lili, Nicole, and I—shared an apartment in Queens, along with my very dear friend Annie. But Stanley would insist I stay with him in Manhattan and limit my time with them. I would try to go to Queens and be with them on the weekends when I could. Often, I stayed with them when Stanley and I had a fight and he kicked me out of his place.

Yet I overlooked these problems as being with him had many more benefits than problems. He was wealthy, had great friends, took me on vacations, and opened up my eyes to the good life. He taught me how to cook Italian food, speak better English, and about American culture and so much more.

In some ways, he was selfish too. For instance, although he owned a few restaurants in Manhattan, he never let me work for him or help me find a better job. Perhaps in a way I was a trophy for him because of my youth and attractiveness. I never felt that he was in love with me. Afraid of losing him, I did my best to be complacent. I never complained, and for the most part I did what he wanted. For example, when he wanted us to go away, I would change my work hours to fit his schedule.

Even when things were good, a part of me was unhappy and unfulfilled. Though our life together was mostly good, he made it crystal clear that he would never marry again or totally commit to me. This troubled me greatly. More than anything, I wanted more in life, a family and children and the beautiful house with a white picket fence. I think his ex-girlfriend left for that same reason. He did not want to compromise with anyone.

I tried using all my feminine wiles to make him change his mind, but he was resolute. And his children were a problem. While the boys seemed to accept me, the daughter hated having a young foreigner as her father's girlfriend.

What could I do? I was in love with him despite it all. I stayed and kept hoping to develop a better relationship with the children, thinking maybe this would make him change his mind.

In comparison to my life before meeting him, I felt very lucky. I had a boyfriend, a job, good money, my sisters with me, and a few good friends. I was living the American dream. People say that everything happens for a reason, and I believe Stanley coming into my life proves this. Without him, I don't know how I would have survived in the US, and as it turned out, in other countries as well.

Back to Romania

It had been another six months since I had returned to the US from Romania again, and on August 31, 1997—the day Princess Diana was tragically killed—I had to return to Romania once more to renew my visa. The trip was fine with me as I got to see my grandma again. I told her about my new boyfriend, Stanley, and even told her how old he was. Twenty-four years older than me, he was almost my father's age. She didn't seem shocked but just asked if I was happy. I said I was, and she said that was all that mattered. She told me to make sure he treats me right and understands who I really am. Wisely, she pointed out that because I come from a different background, he might not always understand me. She was always such a clever lady. That was also the last time I saw her before she passed away. I wish I had told her how much I loved her and I wanted to spend more time with her. If only I had known what was in store for her.

In the beginning of January 1996, I was I riding the subway back to Queens. I had just finished work and was going to stay with my sisters. It was around 10:00 p.m., and I was chatting with my sisters on the phone about what Stanley and I had done for New Year's Eve.

Lili suddenly said, "Something has happened, and I want you to stay calm."

"What?"

"Mamaia died."

Oh my god. My wonderful grandma! "How?" I asked in shock.

There was no explanation for it: she was sixty-seven when she was murdered by her twelve-year-old grandson, my youngest cousin. We don't know why he did it, but it is clear that it happened because he never had a good education. This cousin—I don't even want to say his name—was the youngest of five boys. His parents were busy working a hard farm life, so their children had next to no attention or opportunity for education. He and his siblings all dropped out of school very early. They must have been around ten years old. They had probably only taken maybe four classes, equivalent to a fourth-grade level in the United States, and they continued to spend the rest of their time helping on the farm with various chores. Their parents, I am sure, did not care that their children had left school. This boy was the son of my grandma's middle son. My uncle had five boys, and their mother, a woman who focused on her appearance and little else, had scant interest in bringing up children or caring for her husband. My grandma would complain about her to my uncle. But he was a weak man and did nothing about it.

When he was twelve, my cousin went out with one of his friends into the small town where they lived. It was December 30, 1995, and just after midnight. He got drunk and decided to go to my grandmother's house to ask her for food. She told him to come back another time; it was an incredibly early hour of the morning and freezing cold outside. He begged for her to open the door just to get some water to drink. When she did, he pushed his way inside and attacked her. He started beating her and then decided to rape her. She was strangled under his hands.

We heard afterward that he still had his friend with him. This friend also took part in the rape. We learned these details from him, but who knows exactly what happened that night. She was discovered the morning after by one of her children who had stopped by to check on her. My cousin was caught just two days later. He was sentenced to prison for twelve years, but because he was a minor, he served just three years of his sentence. The entire city was shocked by such monstrosity. I didn't find any of this out until later, almost two weeks after it happened. I felt sick to my stomach when I heard. He was a monster. He had no reason to do what he had done. I could never see him after that. I hope I never get to see his face again as long as I am alive.

My sisters and parents hadn't wanted to tell me about her death as they knew how much it would upset me, and a whole week had passed since her funeral. I was devastated. I cried and screamed on the phone the entire train ride home.

It's been eighteen years since this happened, and when I visit Romania and my uncle, I still refuse to see my cousin. I never wish to see his face again as long as I live. I don't know how I would react if I saw him again. I loved my grandma so much, and she did so much good for us, her grandchildren. To die the way she did made no sense.

CHAPTER 3

An Unexpected Setback

Bahamas, 1996

When I returned to the US after my second trip to Romania, I became obsessed with my weight—something that upset my sisters as I have always been relatively slender. My desire to be skinny stemmed from a fear that, should I gain weight, Stanley might find me unattractive and leave me. He had a thing for skinny women, and before dating me, I knew he had dated some supermodels. He used to introduce me to others as a model, something I detested because it wasn't true, and I hated feeling like a fake. He even used to tease me that I had large cheekbones, a common feature of eastern Europeans, and that when I have children, I would get very fat. He said that my hips and thighs would expand with pregnancy and age. He was wrong about that. I wish I could meet him sometime and show him how wrong he had been. Often, he would squish the skin around my waist and behind and make remarks like, "There's so much meat everywhere." I felt a huge pressure to be skinny and keep up with his expectations.

This focus on me being skinny added to my feelings of not being good enough for him. I would only be happy to improve and be better. I even thought about going back to school to get my GED, but at this time, I was not allowed to because I just had a visitor's visa. Stanley never did anything to help me go to school or to find a better job. He wanted to keep me naive so I would tolerate his lifestyle. These insecurities gave me many nightmares. Still today I have them once in a while. I really want to find him and let him know how much he affected me, but knowing him, he wouldn't care one bit.

Stanley and I had been dating for around nine months, and my birthday was approaching. He offered to take me to the Bahamas to celebrate. I thought this was the perfect timing as my six months of being back in the country was coming up. I had to leave to go somewhere, and I was delighted to not have to leave the country and go back to Romania, especially after my grandma had died.

I wished, of course, that I could just become a legal resident of the US, but this was unlikely to happen because in order to become legal, I had only two options. Find an American husband—and that was never going to happen with Stanley—or get sponsored by an American company, which as I had no special skills wasn't going to happen either.

We left for the Bahamas on June 18 and planned on returning on June 20, my birthday. My sisters and girlfriends were organizing a birthday party for me at my house with our friends upon our return.

Arriving in Nassau, we went straight to Paradise Island, where we stayed at a hotel that is now called Ocean Club. It was my first time being on a Caribbean island, and it was a fabulous experience. The hotel was great, the food was excellent, and I loved the relaxed island lifestyle, especially their slow-talking English accents. The weather was beautifully hot and humid, and the atmosphere was very calming. Little did I know at the time that, just few days later, I would be living there for almost a year.

Stanley and I had an amazing time, and we were disappointed when, forty-eight hours later, we had to leave. We both were in love with everything around us. I had braided my hair in Bahamian style, and we got drunk on the beach. We also had a late breakfast every day and stayed up late both evenings. Even twenty-four years older than me, Stanley and I both behaved like two little children together. We were just nuts about each other the entire trip.

We drove to the airport to return to the US on my birthday. As I went through immigration, I was pulled to the side and attacked with questions. Why was I in Nassau? Who was I there with? How have I supported myself for the last two years in the United States? The visa said I was a tourist with no right to work. Who was the man I was with? What was our relationship? How did I have money to pay rent and other expenses?

I was so frightened with what was happening. Stanley already stepped through customs and was waiting for me at the plane. I didn't know that this could have happened or I would have tried to prepare him. I was scared for my life. I realized very quickly that I might not get back home.

The officers asked me to step aside into a room and to take off all my clothes. A female officer entered the room and started searching my naked body and my handbag and luggage. In my wallet they found a check from a job I had worked before leaving for the Bahamas. That was proof that I was working illegally in the US, and they immediately cancelled my visa. I heard stories from my friends about this happening to others, and now it was happening to me.

I was shocked and terrified. My flight for New York had left, and I assumed Stanley was on it. They told me I was free to go. But *where* could I go? I had no money, and I didn't know anyone in the Bahamas. I was free but stranded on an island. I called my sisters and told them what had happened. This was the second saddest birthday I had, the first was my twenty-first when I had been in a jail cell in Germany.

As it turned out, Stanley was waiting for me outside. What a decent man after all!

As soon as he saw me, he gave me a big hug and told me not to worry. He said he would do all in his power to help me get back to the US, short of marrying me, of course.

He kept his promise, but it took a whole year. In the meantime, I could do nothing but wait. So much had changed in such a short time. That morning we had woken up and were looking forward to going home, and I even had a party to attend—*my* party. By 2:00 p m., I was in a totally different situation. I had no idea what was going to happen or when I would ever be able to go back to the States.

As soon as Stanley and I left the airport, we went back to the hotel and checked in for one more week. He called the US embassy and asked for an immigration lawyer to help me get a visa to stay in Nassau. We were both in disbelief about what had just happened. So much was going through my mind. Now I had lost the visa for the US. What next? Should I have gone back to Romania? And then what? Try to get a new visa again? The immigration officer had told me that it would be a long time before I could ever get a new one. I did not know what Stanley planned to do to help me. I couldn't ask him too much as we had only been together for nine months. It seemed too soon to ask him to do anything for me. What could I possibly have asked him to do? Move to the Bahamas? Take care of me?

God, why did this happen to me? Was it because I left Adrian? Was this my punishment? I just didn't know what the right thing to do was at the time or how to handle it. Fortunately, Stanley came through for me, and he helped me get a lawyer. The lawyer recommended to us was Perry Christie, who would later become the prime minister of the Bahamas. We met over the following two weeks and discussed my options while Stanley and I looked for a place for me to rent.

My options for getting back into the US were so limited. I couldn't get a visa unless someone smuggled me into the country. Take one day at a time, Perry advised. I found an apartment in a decent area and, I took the bus to get around because I didn't have a car. In the meantime, Perry secured me a visa for two months in the Bahamas. When that time was up, I had to go see him and then immigration to renew it.

As hard as it was for me, it's nothing like what it would have been if Stanley had not been there for me. He could have abandoned me but instead chose to stay and help. He paid for everything—the apartment, lawyer, food, clothes—and he made sure I had everything I needed to survive and be happy. All this gave me life and a purpose.

He tried to come to the Bahamas every two weeks or so, and though he was a busy person with three children to worry about, he would stay with me for at least five days at a time, sometimes even for a week.

His mother visited me a couple of times too, and we had an enjoyable time going out for lunch, shopping for lobsters, hanging out at the beach, and going to the casinos. Our fondness for each other made Stanley very happy.

Nevertheless, the situation was difficult. Other than when Stanley visited and the few times his mother came, I had nothing to do and was bored. It was hard to meet people. The building I lived in had only ten apartments, and they were rented mostly by vacationers. It was a wonderful location right on the beach, and the place was beautiful inside. I just wished I had someone to share it with. But we can't have it all, can we? My sisters could not come to visit me as. Once they left the US, they would not be able to legally return. That would have put them in the same situation as me. Paradise felt more like living in a sandy jail. Time dragged on.

Our lawyer finally concluded that the only way for me to get back to the US was to return to Romania and to try to get a different visa from there. Which seemed like a stupid plan because I was already on the US Immigration database. But anyway, I left for Romania about three months after I got stuck in Nassau. It was a waste of money and time. I know that now. An act of desperation that just brought more complications.

Back to Romania Again

I left the Bahamas and returned to Romania. I was miserable. Divorced, no visa for the US—I had nothing going for me and no idea how I was going to mold the future I wanted. I tried to be optimistic, but it was hard.

I got the idea to change the name on my passport from my married to my maiden name in the hopes that they might grant me a new visa for the US. No such luck. They had my fingerprints and refused to reissue me a visa. To get one, I would first need my divorce papers.

I asked my sisters to send me the divorce papers from the US. There were more surprises to come now that I never would have expected: the US Immigration wouldn't accept the papers. My US divorce was not recognized in Romania because no legislation existed between the juristic courts in Romania and the US. As far as Romania was concerned, Adrian and I were still married. I got married in Romania and had to be divorced in Romania too.

I was stuck again. The Romanian lawyer I had in New York had been a fraud. I had thrown away my money on that divorce. I had to start from zero and apply for another divorce again in Romania.

Adrian was not in Romania at that time, and his mother came to court in his place. His family were upset with me. I didn't care. I just wanted the divorce finalized once and for all to get my passport and to get out of Romania. I had been back in the country for two months I was sick of it. So much money had been spent on lawyers, courts, the passport office, and so on, and it was money that I didn't have. I had no idea how or when I was going to be able to make more. Fortunately, Stanley did not abandon me then either. I am forever grateful to him for through those hard times that he stood by me. We had kept in touch over phone calls—at that time, there was no email communication and no cell phones. Even using the phone was an ordeal as my parents, with whom I was now living, didn't even have a phone. I had to visit my neighbors to make a call or go to the post office and have Stanley call the phone there.

Stanley was trying to help me to get a marriage visa and go back to the US with him. But his lawyer advised against it. And so though he had promised to come to Romania to get me, he never did. I felt abandoned, alone, insecure, and unloved. That was my last chance to get my visa back, and when he refused, that was it for me. I had to get out of Romania. I could not stand it anymore. The pressure from my parents about my unfortunate situation was too much. I felt so depressed that I had to get out of there before it was too late for my mental state.

But I don't give up easily. I weighed all my options and decided my best bet was to return to the Bahamas and somehow figure out how to get back to the US from there. Romania did not have a Bahamian embassy in Bucharest, but the English embassy represented the Bahamas, and there was an English embassy in Budapest.

I dreaded the thought of going back to that office to ask for a visa. I did not want to go to the English because, honestly, I was scared of being refused yet again. And if that had happened, then my last chance of returning would have been destroyed. I booked a ticket to Havana, Cuba, as they had a Bahamian embassy there. I felt that I had a better chance this way. I didn't need a visa to get to Cuba as they were also a communist country. Stanley had wired me the money I needed to purchase my ticket and for a hotel. I said my goodbyes to my parents and left once again.

Cuba, 1998

I left for Cuba in September 1998. From Bucharest, I flew to Madrid, and from Madrid to Havana. What an amazing journey. People on the plane were carrying live chickens, turkeys, and ducks in their luggage! I had never seen anything like that before.

When I arrived in Havana, they asked why I was in the country.

"To visit," I replied.

"Why?" they pressed, "I'm writing a paper for my university, and I want to describe the two types of communism. I'm from Romania."

They let me through, but then they also asked where I was staying. I froze.

"I don't know, a hotel?"

The officers looked at me a moment and then asked me exactly which hotel. That was when I realized that I had forgotten to book one. To my salvation, I had met a young man whom I had chatted with on the plane. He saw me struggling with the Cuban immigration officers, so he came to my assistance and told them I would be at the National Hotel. That was the number one hotel in Havana then.

I ended up staying at the National for a few days, but after that I moved to a less expensive one when I found out that I was going to be in Havana for a while. The young man from the plane became my guide and helped me by giving me many other good pieces of advice while I was in Havana. Looking back, I feel like I always had an angel watching over me, no matter where I was.

By this time, I was multilingual. To stay in Germany, I had learned passable German. To stay in France, I had learned passable French. To stay in the US, I had learned passable English. I might not have finished high school, but I now knew four languages, including Romanian. But now I was stuck in a country that spoke Spanish, and I knew not a single word. But here I was, and I would do whatever I needed to survive.

Havana was a very old, beautiful, Spanish-style city. But in spite of their lovely architecture, the buildings were, as in all communist countries, run-down and badly in need of fresh paint. To make it worse, the heat and humidity had added an unpleasant smell to the town.

Supplies were scarce, and the shops were empty: there was nothing to buy. For food, the shelves mostly had local fruit. Even buying toothpaste was a task. If you wanted to have toothpaste, you needed to buy it in hotel boutiques with American dollars as it was only available for tourists. On days when the stores got more eggs and sugar, people came running from every direction and a huge line formed. It reminded me so much of the Romania where I had grown up. This made me sad.

Blond and fair-skinned, I stood out as a foreign tourist, and children sometimes followed me down the street and asked for money or chocolates. I didn't mind. I loved Havana. Though run-down, it was exciting, and the people were nice, kind, and romantic. In the evenings, they lounged around the ocean, singing and dancing. They loved playing the guitar and other instruments and just sitting on the long boardwalk, serenading one another. It was really magical. I had never seen so much love and romance in the air before. Those people were really happy.

After applying for a visa for the Bahamas, I was told to come back to the embassy in two weeks. I didn't have enough money to stay in a nice hotel, and I was afraid of staying in a local hotel as my youth and blond hair might make me a target for thieves. It's not that the Cuban people appeared dangerous. They were actually quite nice to me. It was my state of mind. I was confused and petrified, constantly worried because I didn't know whether I would be given the visa or sent back to Romania.

Stanley was unable to send me money because he was an American and this was a communist country. We spoke every few days, but he was hesitant to get involved as he did not know the ramifications of a US citizen in doing so. I decided to move to a very small local family-run hotel.

The hotel was cheap and disgusting. There was no hot water except for two hours in the evening a few days a week. Sometimes there was no electricity and lots of cockroaches. It was worse even than Romania. But the people were so nice and loving to one another. I believe they were just generally people who liked to enjoy themselves no matter the situation. I could not stay in my hotel room for too long as it was terrible, so every day I found different destinations to journey to. I enjoyed my daily tourist explorations, and I could have easily settled in my new life, but I was scared about the possible refusal from the Bahamian embassy.

The food in Cuba was really good—all homemade and tasty. I discovered a market where they sold just fruits and vegetables, whatever was in season. It was kind of a show. Every day I went there to talk to people and to learn more Spanish. They were the best fruits I had ever tasted. For the rest of the day, I went to visit anywhere that was available to visit. They have beautiful botanical gardens and some really nice churches. I reached out to my friend from the airport, and he helped me by making different suggestions to where I could visit next. He invited me for lunch and introduced me to his family, his mother, his girlfriend, and his other friends too. He lived in Madrid for a few years while he was studying, so he was very knowledgeable when it came to Europe. We spoke in English, thank God. My Spanish then was almost nonexistent.

I also admired the artists painting on the streets. There were ladies dressed up in very festive Cuban attire, and people rolled cigars on the street. There was quite the show every day. I went to the National Hotel a few times for cocktails and dinner, where I met another young family. The couple were both my age, and I met up with them every few days. They showed me around and took me to local places they knew. I managed to have a bit of fun during my exile there while waiting for my Bahamian visa to arrive. Finally, after a tense month, I was given the visa, and I left for Nassau. I felt blessed once again.

Back to the Bahamas

When I touched Bahamian ground again, it felt almost like coming home. Stanley, whom I hadn't seen for three months, met me at the airport. I collapsed in his arms. Safe again!

Although we had managed to speak daily while I was in Cuba, we had the best few days catching up from our lost three months. We felt even more in love than when I left. I had been mad with him when he couldn't come to Romania with me, but he was the one who had suggested Cuba as an option, and he had sent me cash and the plane ticket. Even though he didn't come through for me by coming to Romania, he continued to help me get back to the Bahamas. He was scared that getting engaged for the visa would encourage me to think he wanted to get married again. Even though he made it clear he did not want to get married, he was very caring and sweet with me for the entire time he stayed with me in Nassau. I was naive enough to put my feelings and needs aside to stay in a relationship with him anyway.

We rented a three-bedroom apartment so that his children had the option to visit, although they never did. Nassau can be dangerous, but the apartment was in a nicer area and in a gated community with swimming pools and tennis courts. It felt safe, so I didn't feel worried. It was also close to a supermarket and a few other shops. Nassau had small buses, and they were cheap to hop on and off, but the problem with them was that they were very unreliable. At the time, I wasn't driving, so the location was convenient to me.

I also bought a bicycle so I could go back and forth easily from the shops to the gym and back home again. I loved to exercise, so that kept me busy every day for the entire morning. If I hadn't been able to spend my mornings exercising, with all the time I had on my hands, I might have gotten in trouble somehow.

It was December, and we spent Christmas and New Year's Eve together. After that, Stanley went back and forth to the States.

I tried to keep myself busy when he wasn't there. I went to town, to the beach near our place, and joined the gym. I made a few friends, whom I would sometimes meet for lunch or a Sunday barbecue. I tried not to go out much in the evenings as Stanley was worried about the danger of me staying out later than 8:00 or 9:00 p.m. He could get possessive and jealous, and I think he also worried that I might start dating someone else while he was gone. It was difficult. I am grateful to him for standing by me through it all. He didn't run away like other guys most likely would have done. I went through some costly challenges before getting stuck in the Bahamas, and he had stayed with me even though we had been together for just nine months at the time. I respected him tremendously for that. And he was a gentleman. I gave him 100 percent of my heart, but I felt that he could only give me half of his. The rest of our relationship was built on mutual respect, and that worked for us at the time because I was so vulnerable.

Time went by, and in June, almost a year since I came to Nassau for the first time, Stanley asked if I wanted to try to come back to the US illegally. I needed desperately to continue my life. Just staying on the island and hoping things would happen to make me feel alive again was torture, so I said yes! Of course! I needed to move in some direction.

After I agreed, he called me one evening and said, "Tomorrow you are packing just what fits in a small bag, and you will meet someone at Freeport. Make sure you are there on time, and don't tell anyone what you are about to do." And that was it. I left the next day.

I should have said no.

I took a boat to Freeport, where I met a man who explained how, the following day, we would be flying in a small plane to a small airport near Fort Lauderdale. It sounded straightforward and simple. I went up to my room, but I barely slept a wink that night as I could only think about getting back to New York and seeing my sisters again. I was doing push-ups and squats in the room to make myself tired and to stop thinking about the next day. I finally fell asleep and dreamed about my sisters and Stanley.

The next morning, I met the man again at a private airport, where we boarded a small plane that he would fly. He was a very nice man in his fifties, and he seemed to know what he was doing. I hadn't asked him if this was the first time he'd done this, but I imagined he had some experience. I was shivering inside with mixed emotions. I knew I wanted to get out of Nassau, but I was also scared of what taking this trip would mean. First of all, I don't like flying at all. Second, this was an extremely small plane. I did not know this man at all, so the entire trip sounded all the more terrifying. On the other hand, I had to trust Stanley. I never asked Stanley how he had met or heard of this pilot. To go through with the plan, I needed to be a little crazy—luckily, I was, and so we did it. Hopefully my guardian angel would follow and protect me this time as well. I needed it. Shortly after, I found out that God had different plans for me.

We got into the four-seater small craft. Being in such a small airplane was even more terrifying than getting caught trying to get back into the US. All I could focus on was staying alive until we landed.

I sat next to the pilot in the front passenger seat and counted the seconds. He told me to put on headphones. I could hear him talking to the tower control. They discussed taking off and so on. It was surreal, and the noise inside the plane was so loud. I felt like I was stuck inside a large bumblebee.

It was so beautiful up in the skies. I was scared to even breathe but still I was mesmerized by the stillness and the peace up in the clouds. Unfortunately, our peaceful, quiet flight got interrupted by tower control. About fifteen minutes before we were due to land in Fort Lauderdale, the lady from the tower reported that all planes must land as soon as possible. The winds had changed, and a bad storm had formed, and we were directed to the main international airport.

We looked at each other worriedly. The pilot was agitated. I asked him what was wrong. He asked tower control for permission to land a little outside the airport, but she refused right away. I knew then that I was going to get into trouble. He said he was sorry—this was going to be terrible for both of us. There was nowhere to run or hide. He would get in trouble for giving me a ride illegally into the US, and I would get into trouble for not having a visa to enter. His fear made me even more nervous.

When we landed, we both had to go through customs. As I had no passport, I lied by saying I had gone on a ride with this man, whom I had just met for fun. I had no idea he was going to take me to the US. My attempt didn't work. We were both arrested.

After spending a few hours in a cell at the airport, I was released. Stanley had paid bail to the authorities. They took my fingerprints and my photograph. They asked me not to say anything or I would end up in jail right away. It is considered a serious crime to enter the country illegally. I just could not believe where I was again. I hoped it was all over now forever. But I was in trouble with the immigration even more than before. I had two choices: I could return to the Bahamas or go back to Romania. I chose the Bahamas, and Stanley paid the fare for the plane back to Nassau. A few hours later, I was back in Nassau.

The authorities had given me a ten-year ban on returning to the US. I could not apply for a visa for ten years. I signed all the papers they gave me, devastated at this news but relieved to at least be free to return to Nassau and not put back in jail. I hadn't realized then how badly I had hurt myself and my chances of coming back to the US by doing that. For some reason I considered it just bad luck and let it go. Unfortunately, it wasn't until seven years had passed that I realized the gravity of the situation.

As soon as I landed in Nassau, I was arrested at the airport by Bahamian customs. This time I had no visa to enter, so they held me in a cell in the airport jail. I was mortified. I told them the name of my lawyer, but it was Saturday and almost midnight and they couldn't reach him. I spent the night and almost the entirety of Sunday there until they finally reached him and freed me twenty-four hours later.

I felt cursed, distraught, and scared. Why was I such an unlucky person? All the money that Stanley had spent to get me out was wasted. I went back to my apartment, and my lonely routine with no plans or hope for the future or for ever leaving that island. I felt trapped in a very beautiful cage in paradise.

Stanley called that evening. He was very upset. "Stay calm," he told me. "Something might come up very soon." His hints made me feel excited and hopeful again. But I was still so upset and felt so down. My emotions were constantly changing. I was sure that I would never have another chance to get into the United States. I started hating the Bahamas even more just because I couldn't see a way out of this entire mess. Stanley encouraged me in the best ways he could through the phone. He was not able to come down, and it was probably better he didn't because he was still upset that he had lost all the money on the plane and then on lawyers trying to get me out. He did mention that we would try again sometime soon, not to worry.

A few days later, Stanley called and said to go right away to Freeport again. Someone would be at the main marina waiting to take me fishing. He gave me the name of their boat and the size. I also had the phone number of the man who was going to help me. Stanley told me to put my most important and precious things into a bag. All this happened with less than twenty-four hours' notice. I was thrilled that he had another plan, but this time I was even more scared than before. That was all I knew.

I was still young and very desperate. In spite of the fear of getting caught, I was still ready to try to get into the States again, even if getting caught meant I would face another arrest. Anything was better than sitting around with nothing to look forward to but Stanley's visits every few weeks.

The next morning, I took the ferry to Freeport. I went to the largest marina and met up with my new companions for the next six or so hours. It was just me and two guys, and we left for our fishing adventure. The boat was about twenty-eight feet long—very small compared to what I had imagined. I hate boats unless they are huge. Because I only learned how to swim when I was in my thirties, I had a terrible fear of drowning. But I set aside my fear, and wearing a bathing suit and a nice cover-up, I went along with our fishing adventure.

Over the six hours we spent on the boat, we caught lots of marlins and other fish, a total of maybe fifty, and it was actually fun. We had to stop many times and chat with other boaters and people who were fishing just like us. Everyone was very nice. The most surprising part to me was that I actually got carried away fishing and for a while I forgot about the reason I was there.

We approached the Florida coast and went straight into a private club in Fort Lauderdale. The guards working at the club asked if we had caught any fish, and they were impressed when we showed them how many we had. No problems and no other questions asked.

We got into the marina and anchored the boat. I couldn't believe it. I was actually in the US. I made it back to my family and was close to being free again. In a way, it was so easy to get in but so stressful to finally get our mission accomplished. The past didn't matter anymore now that I was in.

A man was waiting for me in a car outside the marina, and we drove into town. I stayed overnight with a friend of Stanley's, and the next morning I took the train straight to New York. His friends were very nice. We had met them once before when we had come down to Florida on vacation. They were a couple, and what attracted us to them was that they had the same age difference between them as between me and Stanley, and we remained friends. I guess Stanley had asked them if they could help me to get in once I had gotten stuck in the Bahamas because these friends were locals in Florida. It turned out Stanley always knew the right people. They suggested we go out for dinner to celebrate, but I was so paranoid that something might go wrong that I told them I would rather stay in and eat, just to be safe. I did not want to take any chances and be sent back to Nassau. The couple had a small baby now, so I did not want to get them in any trouble either. Even when I stayed the night in their home, I was scared that someone might still find out where I was and come to arrest me. There was no train available to take me to New York that evening. Otherwise, I would have taken it. The husband took me to the train station the next morning and wished me all the best on my new adventure.

It took twenty-four hours to get to the city by train. Excited to see my sisters and my friends again, I couldn't sleep and lay awake staring at the ceiling, making plans for the future and writing in my diary. The economy-class seats on the train from Florida were not the most comfortable, but my mind was already racing ahead, so I didn't mind. I started doing squats and lunges, push-ups and abdominal work, jumping jacks too. There were not many people around me and next to no one in the back of the train. I needed to do this sometimes to tire myself out and shift my mind-set from worrying. It doesn't always work unfortunately. After a long and tiring journey, I finally arrived back in New York.

When I arrived in the city, Stanley was waiting for me at the station. With a big smile on his face, he handed me a huge bouquet of flowers. We held each other tight. From all the stress of the past two weeks, I had lost around ten pounds, which made him even happier. We decided to go out for lunch and plan the new exciting future we had ahead of us. After all, we knew each other for just ten months before I had gotten stuck in the Bahamas. Then we spent one year of our relationship together there because I had no other choice. Now that I was back in New York, I wasn't sure if we would continue living together or if I would go back to living with my sisters. In the end, he invited me to live with him in the city. I was thrilled then, but I regretted it later.

After lunch, I took a taxi to Queens to see my sister Lili. What a joy to be with her and freely walk the city streets again. You truly don't know what freedom is until you lose it. Lili, my sister, had been seeing someone new for about a year, and the two of them had moved in together. He had opened a pizza place in a big mall in Queens, and she was spending her entire time there running the place on her own. I was amazed how comfortable and secure she was with her job and responsibilities. It was so good to see her doing well. We ate pizzas and calzones and chatted for a few hours. I also went to visit my girlfriend Annie. She was doing well, and it was nice to see her and catch up.

My sisters and I were so lucky to be in America. Being back after all this time, I felt like I was flying over everyone; it was an out-of-body experience. There aren't many times in life you get to feel that way, and I was honored to be living it. When I returned to the city that night, Stanley took me out for a beautiful dinner with a dear friend of ours to celebrate. The entire night we held hands and just could not keep our eyes off each other.

For a month after I came back, our relationship was great, but then it went downhill. Stanley's daughter had been staying in his apartment and was not happy to have me back. He was getting migraines almost daily and backaches, too, all of which made him very tired. After finishing work at around 6:00 p.m. and catching a quick dinner in his favorite Upper Eastside restaurant, he was in bed by around 9:00 p.m., and this left us little time to spend together.

Things were better on the weekends. We often went away to Woodstock, where it was so beautiful and very relaxing. We cooked, listened to music, shopped, and rested. During the winter, we went for long walks through the mountains blanketed with snow, and we enjoyed the fresh air. We would cut wood for the fire and lie in front of the fire place, with the smell of burning wood, Frank Sinatra singing, and a glass of red wine. It was so cozy, and these were some of my favorite moments of our time together.

His children were there almost every weekend with their friends. Stanley didn't have any help with cleaning or taking care of the house. I guess he had me for that. We worked hard to keep all the kids happy and busy, and this involved a lot of cooking, making beds, washing clothes, and setting the table for meals throughout the day. I don't remember Jennifer, his daughter, ever expressing thanks for it. His older son, Jackson, was sweet though, and he appreciated what I did.

I put up with all the work and his daughter's distaste for me, and it was emotionally exhausting, causing friction in our relationship. When I would return to New York after spending time with his family, I would tell my sisters how hard it was for me, and they would tell me to leave him. And my sisters weren't the only ones. Stanley had a driver in the city, a nice Polish man with three kids. Occasionally we would speak, and at times he, too, hinted that I should leave Stanley.

But of course I didn't listen. I couldn't. I was too grateful to have someone there for me, and I felt like I owed Stanley for taking care of me through the hard times I had in the Bahamas. Aside from the issues I had with his daughter, Stanley also had a few other habits that I did not like at all. Occasionally he would smoke a little pot, and every few weeks I found that he took cocaine. Those were more recent habits, and I just did not enjoy being with him when he engaged in it. Thank God he was not doing drugs on a daily basis, but at least one weekend a month was consumed by him just suffering the after effects and recovering in bed. After each time, he would be out for at least two days. It was also very unorthodox for me to be part of this behavior. I tried smoking pot a few times, but it just wasn't for me, and eventually I told him that I would leave him and stay with my sisters if he was going to keep doing this. He was so selfish he didn't care at all. I said that hoping to scare him and stop him from doing it again, but it didn't work. Often, I felt like I was wasting my youth and my time by staying with him. He never even gave me a key to his apartment. The entire time we were together and dating, I was always left waiting in the lobby. I loved him, but my joy was always mixed with a kind of sorrow. I felt used.

Yet I always knew there was no future between us. I wanted desperately to get married again and have children. But he not only said that he would never marry me—he also made it clear that he wanted no more children. In fact, during the last two years of our relationship, I got pregnant twice and both times had miscarriages. It must have been God's way of showing me things were not right.

All this as well as other issues infuriated me. And of course, there was always the twenty-four-year age gap to think of. Still, I felt stuck.

Marriage

After two years of being back in New York, I felt my only choice to become a legal citizen was to marry an American. It hurt me that Stanley never wanted to be more helpful in getting me legalized and feeling safe in the US. On the one hand, he told me he loved me; on the other, he could have so easily helped if he had wanted. He had the money, power, and resources. He just never bothered because I guess he loved that I was so insecure all the time and vulnerable to him. If I had been stronger and more independent, I would never have stuck with him and accepted his behavior.

One summer, I met a man named Antonio through mutual friends. Antonio was born in Puerto Rico but had lived in the US for most of his life. He was a hardworking guy and had big dreams for his future, but he had some trouble with his ex-girlfriend because they had a child together, and it was difficult to work, to be single, and to try to take care of his son on his own. We talked often and formed a strong, although platonic, bond that was genuine. He asked me to consider marrying him so that we could solve each other's problems. He knew I was in a relationship with Stanley, but he said that our problems were bigger than that and could be fixed with an opportunity like this.

All in all, it was great because Antonio was such a sweet man and we continued to be great friends—taking pictures together, going out together to talk about our issues—but he did have a lot of baggage. He was very upset about his situation, and I tried to help him and make him feel better, but he occasionally got into trouble with his friends and his ex. He would call me to ask for advice, but he was young and immature for his age. I suppose we both felt sympathetic to each other's situations, but in the end we weren't able to help the other as much as we had hoped.

My life with Stanley had hardly changed through all this, nor did he want to know anything about my marriage to Antonio.

CHAPTER 4

A Second Chance

George

It was the summer of 2001. I had been married to Antonio for just over a year, and I was working as a waitress at La Maganet, an Italian restaurant in Manhattan on Third Avenue. It was just a summer job, and I worked the lunch shift every day. Every summer they opened the terrace and hired extra waitresses to work outside, and I enjoyed working there. The owner was an old Italian man who was very nice to his employees. The staff were also very welcoming, and it was pleasant to work there. The best part about it was that the shift was just four hours at lunchtime and I made good money. I had no idea that there were bigger plans in store for me when I accepted the job there.

I had met some very nice people while working there and even my future husband. Of course, at the time I didn't know he would be the one to give me the love and support I desperately needed. I had met a few of his work partners first. One of them was his boss, and the other young man was one of his colleagues. The boss was married, but his colleague wasn't, and neither was George. Michael, the boss, asked me one day if I was seeing anyone. I said, "Maybe. Why?" He then said, "I have two nice guys here, both available. Which one are you interested in?" I looked at both of them and said, "None of them, actually." I was embarrassed in this moment, so I just left their table and went on working.

A few days later, George, a charming Englishman, returned for lunch. We started to get comfortable and talk to each other more. At the beginning of one of our conversations, he asked me if I had ever dated an Englishman. I told him, "No, but I would like to get to know what Englishmen are all about."

He struck me with charm, and he wore very colorful ties and bright-pink shirts. He was very sweet and funny. Instantly, there was an amazing and new kind of chemistry between us. He came back again over the next few days and offered to exchange phone numbers. I told him, "Sure, but I don't think I'm going to call," because I was already in a relationship with Stanley. I took his number in any case. After work that day, I don't know why, but I called him. It was probably his charm and persistence. We had a wonderful conversation for about forty-five minutes on the phone. He seemed very busy with his work, and he was getting ready to travel to LA for few weeks on business. I didn't invest much into this connection right away because I was still in a relationship with Stanley. I had never before felt attracted to anyone enough that I wanted to end what I had with Stanley. When George kept coming back, I think part of me began to realize then that he was going to be someone special in my life. I loved talking with him, and I instantly smiled and laughed each time we connected. At the same time, I felt nervous, but now I realize what that was all about: it was love at first sight. He was and still is amazing in every way.

After George and I spoke for a while, we said we would be in touch soon and then hung up. Just a few weeks later, George called again. At the time, I was walking to meet Stanley, but I kept George on the phone even as I got to the front of the restaurant where Stanley and I had planned to meet. I saw Stanley inside but still had such a hard time hanging up. We were having a very interesting conversation, and I didn't want to let him go. I had started to realize there was a special energy between the two of us.

I told George my birthday would be coming up soon, and very politely, he asked me which day it would be. When I told him, he said, "Oh no, another Gemini!" I would find out later that George had been in a long-distance relationship with a high school sweetheart on and off for almost twelve years who had also been a Gemini. He swore he would never date a Gemini girl again. He said he would probably be away on that date anyway and also that he was studying to take a test for his job, so it didn't seem like there was much hope for a future between us. I went on with my daily life and work and did not think much about him, but it was just impossible not to. Every few days, he called me again to say hi, but I wasn't always available because I was still living with Stanley.

For my birthday, Stanley took me and his children to Woodstock. It turned out to be a complete nightmare. It became our last weekend together, and from that time I knew I was done with him.

I am a firm believer that everything happens for a reason. My birthday also fell on the same day as Father's Day. I was worried when I saw all the children had brought a large group of guests into the house with them. I was going to be the housekeeper and the cook, *and* it was my birthday. I knew better than to expect any gratitude for it. Still, I could not stop myself from thinking it was a shame about the children's attitudes.

After three nights there, Jamie—his daughter—humiliated me in front of her friends. In front of her father and our guests, she told me that I am not welcome in their house and that she wished I never existed in her father's life. She asked, "Why can't you just go back to the city and disappear?" I was so embarrassed, but this time I was also angry. Stanley was right there next to her, but he didn't even tell her to apologize. Not that an apology would have helped me forget or feel less hurt, but at least it would have helped with the embarrassment I felt. This behavior happened frequently, and I was sick of being abused. I told Stanley to talk to her and to make her stop. He did nothing. I felt so alone. It was always all about his children, and

I would forever be on the bottom of his long list of priorities. I told him I had to go back to the city.

I asked him to drive me home, but he said he was busy. I grabbed my purse and flew out the door, tears running down my face. He didn't even bother trying to stop me.

His house was out in the middle of nowhere, and there were no buses there. Luckily, a car stopped eventually and gave me a ride into town. From there, I took the bus back to the city. It was Sunday, June 20, 2001—yet another very sad birthday. Eventually, after about five hours, I made it back home.

When I arrived back in New York, I rode the subway and decided to call George. We chatted for a while and arranged to meet for dinner later that night. He was back in New York from his trip to LA. I was very pleased to hear that. After all, it was my birthday. When I got home and opened my door, a very large beautiful bouquet of flowers greeted me. From that moment, my entire life changed. I immediately forgot the humiliation I had gone through that morning. Just two hours ago, I felt like my life was over, and suddenly everything felt like heaven. Annie and my sisters were home. They were all very happy for me to be going out to meet George. Everyone helped me figure out which outfit I should wear to dinner, and then we all waited for his friend to arrive to pick me up. We watched the street to see when the car would show up.

I noticed a beautiful black Cadillac limousine with a driver dressed in a uniform complete with a hat. I thought for a second that must be the car I was expecting, but it didn't make sense. He told me his "friend" would be picking me up, but this man was a professional driver. I was confused but kept watching the road. We all did. Then we saw the driver get of the car and walk toward the front door. He rang our bell, and I finally understood this was real. When I asked the driver his name, he said Cummings and that he was working for Mr. George. I was intrigued. At this point, I knew very little about George. In twenty-four hours, I had gone from being down in the dumps to being on cloud nine. It like something out of a movie. I was so nervous but so excited to see what other surprises the evening had to offer. It had gone from being the worst day in a very long time to one of the best days I'd had yet. I was over the moon already, and it had just begun.

We drove to SoHo in downtown Manhattan, and George met me at his front door. We went upstairs into his apartment for just a short time before leaving for dinner. He showed me around the place and then took me to a beautiful restaurant called Barolo. This was our first official date, and we immediately clicked. As we downed a bottle of champagne, I spilled out my life story. I wasn't the least bit hungry and barely touched my food. He still talks today about how I had been so distracted by our conversation that I had eaten a salad with my fingers, something I still can't believe I did. We had such a great time, and there was genuine chemistry between us. It felt so easy to be with him, and I was just relaxed. I wasn't showing off or pretending I was someone else. I was completely myself, and that felt wonderful.

I did end up telling him perhaps too much about my life, but thank God I didn't scare him off. I could feel he was a little amazed by my story, but he kept his cool about it. I had eaten nothing but some green leaves of salad, so I got plastered on the champagne. I was just too busy talking to notice. At the end of the dinner, he bought deserts for me to take home to my sisters and Annie. He was such a gentleman, and that was it for me. I was already in love. I can safely say I did not sleep at all that night. It was all too good to be true.

After that dinner, I decided that I was not going to go run after Stanley anymore. The way I had felt at that dinner was like nothing I had ever felt before. I realized that Stanley was just taking advantage of my situation. Normally I would give him a few days and then beg him to forgive me and take me back, even though whatever usually caused our fights was never my fault. This time I didn't contact him. I wasn't missing him at all. I actually felt disgusted with the entire experience he had put me through. This was the first time in the many years between me and Stanley that I felt strong enough to stand up for myself. I knew the reason for all this, deep in my heart, was George. He made that happen.

As I had broken up with Stanley, I went back to Queens to live with my sisters. I always had my home there. Even though I lived with Stanley most of the time in Manhattan, I had continued to pay rent on the apartment in Queens since my situation with Stanley was always on edge.

All the way home, I was flying, and of course, the minute I walked in the door, I told my sisters and Annie all the details. It had been such a beautiful night. How lucky was I to have met this wonderful man?

George's job required a lot of travel, but when he was in the city, we would see each other a few times a week. Unlike Stanley, he made me feel like the center of his life and treated me like a lady. Our relationship was great.

Two weeks after I had walked out on him, Stanley called to ask if I was okay. I said I was great and told him that it was over between us. He sounded confused and surprised that I had been upset with his family. I told him how his daughter had badly hurt my feelings, how I was upset that he never tried to apologize or even call over the last two weeks to see how I was, and that I didn't want to see him again. This ended our long-term relationship. He was in shock. He knew right away that I had met someone else, and he began to panic. He asked me to meet him for dinner to discuss, and I went. After thinking about it, I felt that I owed him an explanation. In the end, we had spent six years together. And on top of that, I was excited to spill all the good details about this amazing new man in my life. George adored me and treated me with respect and appreciation. I know it was all new and exciting, but there was and still is something very special about us. Even today I feel very fortunate to have met him. Unfortunately, when it came to Stanley, my glass was empty. For the first time since we had gotten together, I was strong enough to say I couldn't try anymore. I had no more energy for that stressful relationship.

George and I continued to see each other whenever possible. In July, he invited me to go with him to the Hamptons for the weekend. I was flattered because I had never been there but had heard all about it. I wanted to go.

He came to pick me up in a very impressive red Porsche. At first, he said the car belonged to his friend but then later told me that he had really bought it that summer to impress me. We had the most amazing ride to the Hamptons. It was just the two of us in the red Porsche, the roof down, both in love, and music drifting through the speakers. I had never been to Sag Harbor before. I had never been before then, but living and working in New York, I had heard about it. George and his friends had rented a house for the season, and it was really something special. It was such a peaceful place, so tranquil and surrounded by nature. There were also small shops and cafés everywhere. We bought fresh fruit and jams and bread. The environment was just so relaxing. I just could not believe that now I was spending time there. I loved it.

George had lots of friends who visited us there almost every weekend. The party scene was wild, and the drinks were always flowing. Some of them were there from England on vacation. His best friend, Johnny, whom he had known since kindergarten, was there. He was very funny, he loved having a good time, and he was very adventurous. Johnny tried teaching me how to swim for the first time and still takes credit for that. As he tried teaching me the techniques, he enjoyed touching my body with the excuse that it was part of the lesson. He was a bit of a player back then.

I was also introduced to George's brother and his sister-in-law, Debra. Debra was so charming and such a happy person. I adored her company from the start, and we became lifelong friends.

It was hard to go back to Queens after two days in Sag Harbor. George dropped me off at the bus station because I had to go back to work, and he stayed for few more days. I felt like my heart was breaking already when we said goodbye to each other. We had spent forty-eight hours together, and we'd had the best time.

But something didn't fit. George kept introducing me as a good friend. We had been together for two months already. He asked me to go away with him to Vale, Colorado, for five days. It would be our first time completely alone together. I said yes without hesitating. Even though George got sick for two days out of the five, we had a wonderful time. It was altitude sickness, so he was on bedrest for those days. Even though this set our plans back, we still managed to have an amazing time. We watched movies and went for little strolls outside. He was very weak and was not allowed to do much exercise if he wanted to get better quickly. We went ice skating and shopping just to get a bit of fresh air every day. We had the good fortune of getting to see a James Brown concert while in Vale. It was an outdoor concert, and I was so overwhelmed with the man. He was a superstar, and I loved his music. I could not believe how old he looked, but his voice was amazing. I remember the night of the concert very well. It was beautiful. It was the beginning of August, but it was still a little cooler late in the evening. We were looking up at the stars and listening to James Brown. It was so romantic. After five days, I was sad to leave George again. Every time we were together, I enjoyed his company more and more. I was just scared that he might not like me as much as I liked him.

After we arrived back in the city, we said goodbye on my front door, and the last thing he said to me was, "Thanks for a fabulous time. We will talk soon." Being away for five days meant he had a lot of work to catch up on.

When we got back to New York, he didn't call me for a while. I think he got scared of how fast our relationship was moving.

On the morning of September 11, 2001, I was home with my sisters getting ready for work. We were chatting over breakfast, and the TV was on. Then it happened. The first tower was hit. We sat staring at the TV, unable to comprehend what we were seeing. Like everyone else, we stayed home for the rest of the day glued to the TV, and we called our parents and friends. It was at once scary and surreal, reminding me of that day we stood in our home in Romania and heard the gunshots outside, then the Romanian leaders being executed. This time, however, I was pretty sure that what was happening would be even more tragic.

I knew that George lived only ten minutes from the towers. I still hadn't heard from him since our trip but decided it was best to call him to see if he was okay. He was happy to hear from me, and we set a dinner date for the next day. I told him I had some pictures that I had taken in Colorado that I wanted to share with him.

We met the following evening and had a great time catching up and talking about our vacation in Vale. He invited me to go the

Hamptons for the weekend, but I had to work. At least we were talking again. We had had almost three amazing months together, and everything had been perfect between us. The only person pulling back was George. He just did not seem ready for what we had. Or at least he was saying that. At this point I wasn't sure what there was left to do. It annoyed me that he had never introduced me as his girlfriend to people we came into contact with or in front of his friends.

Finally I found out he was living with a female friend, Maggie. She was also from England, and they had known each other a long time. This is why I was introduced as a good friend. He wasn't dating Maggie, but it was a strange arrangement. They knew each other through his ex-girlfriend—Maggie had been her best friend, and they had all lived together. When George had broken things off with his ex, Maggie remained in the house with George. The breakup had been fairly recent when I arrived on the scene, perhaps only a few months prior. Maybe George and Maggie would have gotten together if I'd never shown up. At least this was what I thought to myself when I found out about her.

In the meantime, Stanley had occasionally called and was very apologetic about the way he had treated me. I still didn't want to see him and told him I had met someone of whom I had become very fond.

One day, Stanley popped in at the restaurant where I was working. This was quite unlike him. He told me he missed me very much, that he had spoken to his children and they understood how important I was to him. His daughter even wrote me a note saying she was sorry for being hard on me all these years.

After the biggest hug and with a huge smile on his face, he went down on one knee. With a small Tiffany's box in his hand, he asked me to marry him—right in the middle of a busy lunch with me in an apron trying to serve the customers. If I said "Yes," he told me we could drive straight to his lawyer to sign papers stating that we will have one child together. He had it all organized. It sounded exactly what I had wanted for at least the past six years we had spent together.

After all those years of wanting this to happen, I stood frozen, not knowing what to do. I would finally be safe and secure and well taken care of. But I also realized that the proposal was, as always, on his terms—he was *letting* me have *one* child. It felt as if he was making a deal with my life. I told him, "Thank you, but I am in love with someone else." I said this to him with just half of my heart. A part of me was still in love with him. Or perhaps it was just the idea of being married that sounded like everything I had ever wanted. For a moment I wished I had never met George, but then I knew: he was part of my life and I had a great time with him and I felt good being with him. He was my age, very charming, lots of fun, always very gentlemanly, and charismatic. There was nothing left for me to give Stanley. I had to say no, and I actually felt sorry for him. He looked really sad. He was disappointed that he had not respected me more when he had me. Or maybe not. Maybe he just felt like he lost a good deal. The way you might feel in a business transaction. Still, I felt scared and unsure. What if George was not the love of my life? What if after a wonderful summer he would leave me, and I would be heartbroken twice?

Later, after George and I reunited, I told him what had happened. All he said was that he hoped I would not regret my decision later. He wasn't very reassuring in that moment, but of course George could not commit as he was scared to begin a serious relation with someone so soon after his last breakup. I thought about it a lot and remembered that on our first date at Barolo on my birthday he did jokingly tell me that he would marry me one day. He actually called me wifey, and I loved it. I decided to go with my heart as always.

I didn't care what happened. I wanted this man, and I decided I would do all in my power to get him. I told him that I was his and I had no intentions of going anywhere. He laughed because he was not looking for a serious relationship but just to have fun. And we did have fun the entire time we were together.

The more we were together, the more I knew I didn't want to lose him. I let time pass to give him space. I knew my desire for a serious relationship scared him.

While I was giving George space, I called Stanley. We had decided to stay friends. We met for dinner a few times, and at the end of August he invited me, my sisters, and my friend Annie to Woodstock for the weekend. My six-year-old nephew, Alex, Lili's son, had just arrived from Romania for a few weeks, and he came along as well.

One afternoon we were hanging around the pool. Lili, Annie, and I went upstairs to make drinks and lunch while Nicole relaxed on a lounge chair. Alex fell in the water. He couldn't swim, and he started to drown. At that moment, Nicole fortunately got up to go upstairs. She noticed something not moving at the bottom of the pool. Quickly realizing it was Alex, she jumped in and saved his life. Even today we remember that day and we count our blessings with Alex.

We all got on very well as friends, but something was missing now between us. I mean, Stanley had invited me and my family there for a reason. He was hoping we would get back together, but I didn't have feelings for him anymore. I was missing George very much and felt guilty being there. I called George from the house and lied to him, telling him that I was somewhere away with my sisters and there were no phones available to call and talk. He asked where, and I lied again, saying we were in the middle of a park and that I had forgotten what it was called. At first, he was very nice on the phone, but then he became suspicious. After that, we didn't talk again for a few days. I wasn't sure if we were still together or not at this point. He had pulled back from me a lot since our Colorado vacation. He kept to himself, and I was hurt because I just did not know what to make of it. Even so, I was finished with Stanley. Again and again he invited me to go out and talk. Once he even sent me a poem he wrote, apologizing to me for the way he treated me over the six years we were together. I loved what he had written and thanked him, but again told him that I had moved on. In my heart there was only room for George.

New Job and Moving Up

I had been working the outdoor terrace of a restaurant, and now the middle of September, it was getting cool out, and the outdoor section would soon close. I decided to leave, and I quickly got a job as a manager at Café L'Express, a restaurant on Twenty-First Street and Park Avenue. I loved it. It was busy, had delicious food, and attracted very interesting clientele, such as models, actresses, singers, as well as the everyday kind of crowds. What's more, everyone there made me feel welcome, and we had great fun. It was the first time I had done managerial work, and I enjoyed the challenge and responsibility.

George and I were doing great. He would come to the restaurant often and hang out in the evenings. Stanley would occasionally stop by unexpectedly. He was shocked that I had a managerial job as I think he had always had low expectations of my abilities. A part of him was jealous because I was moving up. I was doing extremely well and made lots of friends at the job. I was busy, and I probably looked very happy to him because he kept asking me out to talk.

Eventually I called him from work one day to talk, and he insisted I should come over to his place to chat. I told him a fictional date just to get off the phone, but he took my word for it. He knew that I was in a serious relationship with someone else. George had become more serious with me, perhaps because I hadn't just dropped him and I showed him that I was real and that I cared for him. Through it all, George gave me confidence and support. I finally felt accepted as a person and not just a refugee or second-class citizen. I couldn't believe my luck that someone actually loved me for who I was and respected all my drive and ambition to become a better version of myself. Instead of an obstacle like Stanley, George became a true partner.

George was a self-made success. He had joined a company when it was very young and had already been made a partner in finance by the time we began dating. He believed that anyone could achieve anything if they put their mind to it. I was—and still am—impressed by how incredibly hard he worked, and he always brought this attitude home to our relationship, challenging the two of us to be better as a couple. For one, he encouraged me to finally get my GED.

One day, early on in our relationship, I remember very clearly how he suggested I go to school to get my diploma, and immediately I refused. I was nervous. I had been married to Antonio for close to sixteen months, and I had an interview for a green card coming up. I had received my Social Security number and the right to work about four months after we had gotten married. This was how I was able to get a job as a manager, and it was a tremendous breakthrough in the system for me. It was also the ticket in for me to go back to school if I wanted. After a while, I had given it some thought, and I went to a middle school in Manhattan for six months to do this, morning classes three times a week to take the course. Thank God it was free, so I could actually afford it. I put a lot of work into the GED, especially since English was not my first language. On top of that, I had to learn the history of the United States and even some science. The math I found hard in general, but learning it from an English-speaking teacher was even more difficult. George offered to get me a tutor who came to our apartment in the few weeks before the test to help with math. Luckily, I passed on the first try and was thrilled and extremely proud when I got it. I owe all of it to George because he insisted I try, unlike Stanley who could not have cared less about me succeeding and feeling good about myself.

George also pushed me to get my driver's license. I had never even imagined myself behind the wheel of a car, but again George encouraged me to go. A few of the girls from work were going to get theirs, and they asked if I would come along. Together there were about five of us girls. Thanks to George's persistence, I passed the test first time! It was fun to go with the girls, and finally, I had an ID. I was thrilled. I always had some trepidation about being a passenger in a car.

When I was around ten years old, I had been in a bad accident. The driver that had picked me and my sisters up was young and had only learned to drive a few months earlier. It was December, and the weather conditions in our hometown were bad. The day before had seen a snowfall. It was drizzling, and his car slipped on the road and turned upside down. There were five passengers and the driver. No one got hurt badly, but we were all frightened. The driver was flustered as, being a new driver, his insurance was going to skyrocket, and he wasn't really allowed to take passengers in his car for money. He asked us to get of the car and start walking so we wouldn't get him in trouble when the police arrived. I was afraid to get into a car for a while after that. I still am today when someone else drives. Getting my own license meant I could be in control of the vehicle myself for once.

Finally, after being in the US for so many years, I was able to become a legal citizen, and I started to feel that I had some rights. I was so nervous about the green card interview. Antonio and I both had all the necessary papers prepared. Taxes, pictures, proof of all kinds of things to show that we were a couple and had been living together. We did hear a lot of horrible stories of when others went to their interviews, and the fear becomes larger than the actual truth. But then came a wrench in my plans. It ended up being terrible news for us. We waited patiently in the room until our names were called. When the interviewer asked all the questions we expected, we were right on track with the answers. Because of this, I thought it was going well. After, he listened to us finish talking, then he suddenly said, "It really doesn't matter that you brought all these papers here today. They are all unnecessary in your case. We are not going to let you in this country. Remember how you entered the US the last time? That was illegal. Because of this, we cannot give you your green card. As a matter of fact, you need to get out of the country. If you decide to come back, then we will discuss your options again."

The immigration officer asked me to leave sooner rather than later. I had a maximum of one year to leave on my own. Otherwise, they would deport me. They knew where I lived and worked. Up until this point, I had been in the US for six years. I had not seen my parents or my distant relatives in that time. I was crushed when I heard that news. All my dreams were disappearing right before my eyes. But I was not going to leave the US. My sisters were here, and now I had started a life. Where would I go? To Romania, after all the years I had spent away? After all my struggles to make a future for myself?

I had gone from Germany to France to the US and the Bahamas. I couldn't face going back to square one again. Unbelievable. And—finally—I was in an amazing relationship with George. No way was I going to leave, but what was I going to do? Stay illegally again and keep hiding away? My work permit and Social Security number were not going to work for more than the next three months. After that it would be back to the beginning again. I thought life was so unfair to me. I felt crushed, disappointed, and extremely unlucky.

Because of my situation, Immigration told me either to think about leaving the US or to apply for an appeal. I ended up staying one more year until, tired and fed up of always looking over my shoulder and worrying, I made the decision to leave.

A week or so before Christmas of that last year, George and I decided to move in together. He was still living with his friend Maggie. They were never involved, but because they came from the same town in England and knew each other through mutual friends, they had a great rapport, and living together worked out well for them. The three of us all lived together for a while, and it was fine with me.

Maggie was a woman with high principles, and she looked out for George. She told him to stop buying me presents and treating me like a princess. I believe she felt I was taking advantage of his good nature, and she was a very intelligent girl. She had a similar job to George's as well. They were both in the same kind of business. Because of their interests and careers, the two of them always had plenty to talk about. They more or less had the same friends, and they both loved the good life and having fun. Both being independent and making good money, it was easy to feel like they could end up with each other. But there I was, from a totally different world with so many issues with my past and my papers.

Coming from different cultures is already difficult sometimes for two strangers to navigate and start a relationship. This time it was even harder. Maggie was overprotective of George. They also had a housekeeper, who would take care of the two of them five days a week. She would clean and sometimes even cook. She was also not happy with me being there. She had been very close to George's ex-girlfriend, who had been with him for close to twelve years before I showed up. She was also close to Maggie. I had to prove my honesty, love, and commitment not just to George but also to Maggie and their housekeeper.

Shortly after I moved in, Maggie met a guy from Yugoslavia one night at a disco and they quickly got married. When I say quickly, it really was fast—we're talking just two months and they were married. We were all shocked, and we took that as a sign that she had been upset with George. At first, I think she saw me as a predator and a threat. I was in his life now, and maybe she was rebelling. Maybe she was upset that I had walked into his life and destroyed some possible future they may have had. Now the four of us were living together. It was a very large loft—one open-plan room. George and Maggie split the room to make two rooms and two bedrooms, and of course, we had a bathroom. In a corner of the living area, we had a treadmill and a few weights. While our place was over two thousand square feet, it was too small for the four of us.

George always tells our stories differently than I do. He says that just a month after I met him, I came to his house with a suitcase full of clothes. He says that I told him that I was moving in from that moment. I think it's such a funny way of describing our beginning. What did happen was that I brought some clothes over to have for when I would sometimes stay overnight. Often when I stayed with him, I had to go straight to work in the city the next day. Our stories share traces of the same events, but we have different explanations for them. He still makes me laugh every time he tells his side of that story.

For Christmas that year we moved in together, it was just George and I in the house as Maggie and her husband had gone to Canada. I bought a beautiful huge tree and decorated it. I invited my sisters and nephew over as well as George's brother and his sister-in-law, Debra. We had a wonderful time cooking both Romanian and British food, opening presents and sharing stories.

The New Year started great. I was very happy, in love with a fabulous man, and my sisters were doing well too. But I didn't know what to do about my papers. I still had to watch every step I took, and I was very careful not to get into any trouble with the law. My situation was the same as illegal immigrants from countries like Mexico, who enter illegally and try to stay under the radar and not get caught. Like them, I worked at minimum-wage jobs, mostly in restaurants, happy just to be inside the country.

One thing I did decide to do was to divorce Antonio as our marriage wasn't helping either one of us with our issues. I hadn't seen my parents or left the country in six years and felt that I should visit, but I was afraid that I wouldn't be allowed to come back once I left. Amid all the worrying, the one thing that was truly great was my relationship with George. I was also scared that if I left the country or if I stayed married to someone else, I might eventually lose him too.

At the beginning of March, we moved to our own place. Maggie did not seem to be bothered by all of us living together now. I had grown used to sharing the space, but we didn't have much privacy. Now Maggie was married, but George and I were just dating, so we were the ones to move out. I was relieved not to see the housekeeper and to have to answer her nasty questions. She always pressured me with personal inquiries like, "What's your relationship like?" "Does he buy you things?" "What do you do when you go out?" and I didn't think it was any of her business to ask.

George and I moved to our own place on Thirty-Seventh Street and First Avenue. It was cozy, and we loved it. The building had a gym and a swimming pool. Unfortunately, just as we moved, he found out that he had to travel to Europe for work.

That same month, soon after we had moved in, George had to go to Switzerland for three months. I was left home alone. Sometimes my sisters visited and slept over to keep me company, but otherwise I was lonely. To keep busy, I started going to the gym every day before work. We decided that when the three months of traveling were up, we didn't want to keep renting our place anymore. When George returned, he rented a house for the summer in the Hamptons so we would be there every weekend from Memorial Day to Labor Day and then spend our weekdays in the city. It worked out well.

I also had a great new job working for Jack Sawyer, an attorney. He was a great guy who was very family-oriented, and we are still good friends today. I had met him in the restaurant where I was working when I first met George. He had been having lunch with a client. We started chatting, and he mentioned that he needed an assistant secretary. If I was interested, I should call him. Eventually I did.

In his office, I helped him and his partner with office work. It was a challenge for me. I had to learn to type, go to the bank and deposit checks, order supplies, and other responsibilities. I felt more competent and able to handle life after starting this job—that is, more competent at everything except legally getting into the US.

Summer had been passing quickly, and in June, George decided to throw me a big thirtieth birthday party. We had moved back to the loft we previously lived in as Maggie had decided to move elsewhere. Though huge for the two of us, it felt like home again. My sisters and Romanian friends visited often, as well as some of George's friends and his brother. George and I were comfortable and really enjoying being with each other. Life was good.

George and I spoke to lawyers to see what choices I had to become a legal citizen of the US. I had none. The lawyer said if I left, I should be able to return in around three years. Wrong! It took thirteen.

After much discussion, George and I decided I must leave or else risk getting arrested or deported. We were so sad. How were we going to be together? Though he had to travel to Europe often, his work was mostly in the US.

I was not even sure where I would go. I might not have been born a gypsy, but it felt like I was becoming one.

I will never forget the Sunday the following March when we both decided it was time for me to leave the US. We sat on our bedroom floor trying to plan our life together in Europe somewhere, talking, crying, laughing, hugging, and making love. Returning to Romania seemed best, and we made the arrangements. Lili would also return, and George would come along with us. I felt more reassured that he wouldn't abandon me.

My parents greeted us as we landed at the airport in Bucharest. I hadn't seen them in seven years, and we were all emotional. I introduced them to George, who spoke no Romanian. My parents spoke no English, but as soon as they saw him, they knew he was perfect for me.

That night, we stayed at the Marriott Hotel in Bucharest. It was my parents' first time staying in a hotel, and they were thrilled to go to the pool and eat dinner in a fancy restaurant inside the hotel. Except on special occasions like a wedding or baptism, my parents always ate at home.

My father was furious at the high prices, and as soon as he saw the menu, he started cursing. Why should George have to pay such prices for food that we can buy for a fraction of the cost at a kiosk? Before we left for our rooms, he took everything from the table, including the forks and knives and even the salt and pepper shakers. I was mortified. I had been out in the real world and knew how inappropriate that was. You might say my father was a country bumpkin, but admittedly if that were my first time dining out in an elegant restaurant, I probably would have done the same.

All in all, it was a great evening. We shared stories and had a wonderful time. The next day, we left for Braila and stayed at my parents' house. We took George around the city and showed him the places where we had grown up. We took him to the countryside where our grandma and my mother's relatives lived. The size of the farms amazed him as in Ireland, where he had spent many of his childhood vacations, the farms were small. He especially loved the fruit and vegetable markets.

Never having met a foreigner before, my family was impressed with how kind and sweet George was with everyone. He never stopped smiling. Of course, he was smiling because he didn't understand a word of Romanian!

George enjoyed my family even though his family was very different. He grew up in a happy family, and he and his brothers had many opportunities between them. Their family is close. George's youngest and middle brother both lived in New York as well. His older brother lives in England with his wife and two children, and though George doesn't see them often, they enjoy each other when they do see each other.

His parents were teachers, and although they weren't wealthy, the country had a good education system, and his parents encouraged the boys to study hard and work for good grades. Sports were also important in their lives. George and his two brothers played soccer, rugby, and tennis. Their weekends were spent traveling to where the boys were playing their favorite team sports.

My father asked me about my future with him. Would we return to the US? I said I would be unable to return but that George and I would always be together, though figuring out how would be challenging. He gave me a look and a sarcastic laugh, as if to say, "Fat chance." I worried about us being able to keep our relationship strong but tried to stay positive. I had no plans on where to go to next, but I knew I would never stay in Romania. I thought about going to visit an old school friend in Spain.

Marbella, 2003

I had a good friend from high school that lived in Marbella, Spain. Laura and I had been friends since we were fourteen. It was because of Laura, and after spending a week in Romania, I decided to visit her. My sister Nicole came with me to Spain, while Lili flew back to New York with George.

After arriving in Marbella, Nicole and I went straight to Laura's house. She lived in a small two-bedroom apartment with her husband and son. We slept on the couch, and it was tight living for us all. Screams from the bedroom woke us up in the middle of the third night. The husband was angry about us being there. We left in the morning and got a hotel room. I just could not stay with her any longer. I tried to talk to her about what happened, but she told me that he was just stressed from work and it gets to him sometimes. He is a good man, she said. I didn't think so from what I had seen.

That aside, I loved Marbella from the start and felt I had made the right decision. I never wanted to leave. When I told George about it, he suggested I look for something to rent for a few months. We found a nice two-bedroom apartment in the mountains that was walking distance to Manolo Santana, a great tennis club with a swimming pool. We still go there today when we visit Marbella. It was perfect. Nicole and I loved it, and when he came to visit, George loved it as well.

Marbella was relaxing and welcoming, and we decided to make the city our home. Lili came to visit in July and August with her son, and it was great to have good company for the summer. We went to Manolo Santana every morning, and then we were off to the beach. With such an amazing fitness routine, we were both in great shape.

George came every two weeks and stayed for at least a week each time. When George and I lived away from each other, I suddenly felt very lonely. I was hoping in my heart that the distance of an ocean between us would not mean we would be separated forever. Even though we saw each other every two or three weeks, after he left each time, I would get extremely depressed for the first few days. The time difference put him six hours behind me, so we had created a routine so we could speak on the phone as many times as possible through the day. I would wake him up at 6:00 a.m. every day and say good night to him at 4:00 p.m. his time. Some days I felt like he would meet someone else on his travels that would make life easier for him. I wasn't sure how long we would be able to maintain our long-distance relationship. Fortunately for me, just two months after I left New York, George came back with a big question to ask me.

On July 4, he proposed to me in Marbella. He told me how he much he loved me and how hard it was to be away from me. Thank God he had also fallen in love with Marbella, Spain. He felt at home there right away. He loved the food and the people, and he even enjoyed our small place. He fit right in. Before he proposed, he had come down to visit just twice. We had talked about what we should do for our future. I told him that I could stay in Marbella and he could come to visit as often as possible. "Yes," he said, "but how long we can do this before we get sick of traveling or run out of money?" Then we thought about the Bahamas. I had a history there already. I was not a stranger to the place. This time it would be even better for us because he could come down every weekend. It was not a terrible plan.

The night he proposed, he nervously paced up and down our large terrace with his hands behind his back, holding a small black box in one hand. Finally, I asked him what the problem was. He looked at me and said, "I am ready for this."

He dropped to one knee and asked if I would be willing to marry him. "New York is not the same without you," he told me.

"Of course!" I said yes right away. I had felt his anxiety that weekend. I would be lying if I said that I didn't know he was going to propose to me. I knew in my heart that we were both missing each other insanely, with me in Spain and him in the US. Without getting married, I had no other way to get back to the US, and I could not see how we were going to make it. When he did propose, I was so relieved to have confirmation that he felt what I felt. We shared the same deep sadness and desperation to be together the entire time we were apart.

I felt like the luckiest woman alive. I couldn't believe I would soon be Mrs. George McKone. My friends, parents, and all our family were thrilled. We felt confident that we would figure out how to make things work for us. Even though we still had to say goodbye again a few days later, we felt much closer to each other, like we were finally one unit. We were going to be together for the rest of our lives. We both had made a commitment to each other by saying yes. It was just about finding the right solution for us to get back together in the same country again. And with the help of God, we found a way.

We got married on October 18 in Romania. My sisters came from New York, as did one of George's brothers. All my cousins, uncles, and aunts were there too. Unfortunately, his parents and older brother and his family weren't able to make it. I'm still not sure why they didn't come to our wedding. Maybe his parents were a little upset that I was not Catholic. Or maybe they did not believe our marriage was real. Or perhaps because I was not English or Irish. Whatever the reason, it really doesn't matter now. The important thing is that we are still together and we made it work.

It was a beautiful, very special day that I will never forget. The wedding party totaled about thirty people. After a lovely wedding ceremony in a beautiful cathedral, we all went to a nice restaurant with live music. I wanted to keep everything very traditional and Romanian because we were there and we both thought it was important to honor tradition. Our wedding finished at 6:00 a.m. the next morning. George was amazed with the traditions we have at Romanian weddings and how seriously we took them.

George's family got to know me more after we got married, and they came to another ceremony we had a year later in the Bahamas. Our families got along really well together. His brother came over from England with his baby. His parents were there too. My parents and sisters flew in again, as well as many other friends of ours.

Just two days after our Romanian wedding, we had to leave and go to Ireland in time for Maggie's wedding ceremony. She had done something similar to us in that she had gotten married already—signing the papers in the town hall in New York—and was having a formal ceremony and party later in Ireland with her family. George's trip to Romania coincided with both events perfectly. Maggie's ceremony was to be held at a beautiful castle. It was a very traditional wedding with over two hundred guests, an amazing dinner service, and reception. Everything was very well organized. This was all so soon after I had gotten married in Romania that I felt like I was on cloud nine. George's parents and his brother and sister-in-law were there as well, so I got the chance to party with my new family. I felt honored and lucky to be there. I still felt a little bad that they never came to our own wedding in Romania just a few days earlier, but it was also my first time in Ireland, so I wanted to enjoy every minute of it.

Because her wedding was on November 1, Maggie had organized a Halloween party the night before. It was a weekend of just party after party. Every meal of the day was carefully chosen and organized so that everyone could pick something they would enjoy. The wedding finished in the early hours of the next morning, like ours.

George had to leave just before the wedding finished to catch a direct flight to New York. After all the partying, he was a little intoxicated when he left. He had to drive himself for about two hours to Dublin Airport. He got pulled over by the police because of his driving that morning. He got a ticket, but they eventually let him go. He got very lucky. I left later that day to go back to Nassau.

Bahamas, 2004

As much as we loved Marbella, George and I decided it was best for us to live in Nassau. Nassau was just a three-hour flight from New York where George's office was. As soon as I arrived from Europe, I went straight to a hotel and checked in.

I stayed in the hotel for a few weeks. Right away, I started calling different real estate agents and told them what we were looking for. I found us a small cottage to rent in the very private Lyford Cay community. It was a beautiful three-bedroom on the canal—perfect for the two of us. George traveled back and forth almost every weekend. The lady we rented from was a widow, and she was really lovely. We had everything we needed. I bought a car and started to get out of the house a bit more every day.

Still it was hard for me as I had few friends in Nassau and I was lonely. Soon I started to meet people and socialize, and I felt safe there. I assumed it would be temporary as we were working on my papers for the US. We had no idea it would take us thirteen years! I introduced George to the people that I knew from living there before. We were in our new home for about a year, and we felt really good about our future. After that we decided it was time for us to buy something. We realized it could take us a long time until I was able to get back in to the US, so we wanted to feel more at home.

We bought a house with the most charming garden. It needed repairs but was cozy. We also wanted to have a proper wedding in the Bahamas and set the date for October 25, 2004. I resolved that from June to October I would finish fixing up our house so my family had somewhere to stay on their trip over for the wedding. We took everything out from the original house and just kept the roof. We also expanded and added two more rooms. We replaced the floor tiles and the windows and pretty much gutted the place. It was a lot of work, and my resolution was to finish it all in just three months was insanely ambitious. On top of that, the weather was terrible. Hurricane season is June to November, and there was a very large amount of rain coming through the Bahamas every day. Unfortunately for us, we experienced two major hurricanes there. I had no idea how much work was going to be invested in that home. It was hot and humid outside, and the mosquitos were everywhere. I pushed the workers to hurry up and finish so I could move in. We just had windows put up in the bedroom, and the floor it was not even finished. The toilet was not functioning, and everywhere was messy with construction. But I had lost my patience with them. I started to buy lunches for them daily and made them lots of coffee. Anything they wanted I was ready to provide just for them to finish on time. This was island life, and they moved extremely slowly. Supplies were delayed coming in too. If the weather was terrible, then forget about deliveries. The boats couldn't get in or out if the weather was too stormy. And once they do make it in to the harbor, they still have to go through customs. That could take up to three days to get cleared. It was a long, slow process.

There was a hurricane just two weeks before our wedding. Hurricane Frances hit the major island of Grand Bahama. The vegetation looked terrible, and there was a lot of damage through our island. We were fortunate enough that we did not suffer much damage to our new house and garden. But the workers needed to secure their homes, so we lost about two weeks of progress because of it. The island did not look at her best, but most of the people coming to our wedding had never been to Nassau, so they loved it anyway.

We were tremendously worried and stressed about everything between the weather and then all the wedding preparations on top of that. By the day of the wedding, we welcomed George's parents, his older brother and sister-in-law, my sisters and parents, as well as George's friends and even some clients from work. We had about eighty people there. In our house we had around twelve adults. People were sleeping all over the place. We didn't have enough bedroom space to house everyone, but somehow we all squeezed in and made it work. The house was still under construction. My bedroom was done, but I had no bathroom. Despite this, we made the best of the time with our guests.

Our wedding was on the beach at a club called Old Fort—the perfect scenery and a huge success for us and our guests. It was a very old, privately owned club. It was situated on one of the most beautiful beaches in Nassau. The clubhouse was stunning. It has lots of charm and character. The beach stretched for about 1.5 miles each way. The sand felt just like flour, and the sand was a light golden color. The water was stunning. No matter what the weather was like, that water continuously changed colors and was always so inviting.

We had a live band for the entire evening. The best one on the island at the time. It was truly amazing. After the priest finished the ceremony at the church, we drove golf carts in a long chain over about eight over to the club. We made as much noise as possible, and it was just so funny to see this long chain of small golf carts all decorated driving to the club. Every single person who came said they had the best time ever. The food, the scents of the plants, the beach, and the company who all got together created an exceptional evening for us. The next day George had organized a golf tournament for the people who were interested in taking part on the famous Lyford Cay. After golf, we all met for brunch at the beach club inside the Lyford Cay community. Again, we had a wonderful time. Everyone behaved and got along well. Most of our guests came for five to seven days, so we were able to spend time with them daily.

After the wedding, we tried for a baby, and I got pregnant immediately with twins. Unfortunately, at ten weeks, I lost one of the babies. The other still had a heartbeat.

I was torn apart and went to see a doctor. For the first time, I found out that I had a bicornuate and reversed uterus. A bicornuate uterus is shaped like a heart with two horns, and the inside wall is partially split. This made pregnancy difficult. I didn't know if I would be able to have children, and I was devastated. The doctor in the Bahamas advised bedrest the next time I got pregnant, along with tying my uterus. That involved a small procedure but increased my chances of not losing the baby. He also said that I should look for a specialist in high-risk pregnancies who would perhaps give me better advice.

I had a friend in London who booked an appointment for me with a specialist over there. At this time, I still had one baby with a heartbeat and another one dead inside my womb. I was stuck and not sure what to do.

I decided the best thing was to fly to London and see this English specialist in high risk pregnancies. I left Nassau a few days later, and by the time I got to the specialist, I had lost the second baby. He told me exactly what the doctor in Nassau had said. Needless to say, I was terrified to get pregnant again.

I had to have a dilation and curettage procedure. In London, they wanted to charge over 2,500 pounds for this—an exorbitant amount—as I didn't have private insurance there. I decided to go to Marbella for the procedure, where it turned out to be free. I went to the main local hospital. The date was December 22, and I was on my own as George was still in New York. They kept me in overnight, and the next morning I went back to my apartment. I rested one more day and left for Cortina d'Ampezzo, Italy, to meet George for Christmas. The amount of courage I had was unbelievable. I had to go through all this alone. I did so much flying and seeing doctors all on my own.

I felt so sad over the loss of our baby. I had never lost a baby this way, and the first one hurts the most because of the fear of not getting pregnant again. I had just had surgery, and the doctor told me to rest up. I was happy to go and meet up with George and spend Christmas together in the Dolomite mountains. George thought that going skiing would cheer me up. Of course, right after a procedure wasn't an ideal time, but I really wanted to change my mind-set.

When it came to skiing, I was a terrified beginner. By accident, George and I found ourselves face-to-face with a black slope for advanced skiers. As there was no way I could ski down that treacherous slope, I slid down on my butt and cursed George the whole way. Whenever I looked down, I felt sick to my stomach. By the time I got back to the hotel, I was bleeding heavily, and I had to stay in bed for the rest of the trip.

Nevertheless, Italy was breathtaking. The food was mouthwatering, and everyone was so beautifully dressed that I actually did enjoy myself. We got lucky on that trip with the snow too. By the time we were due to leave, there was so much snow that we were delayed. We had finally got a different flight and went back home to the Bahamas.

A few months later, I was overjoyed to find out I was pregnant again. At twelve weeks, I had not lost the baby, and I went to Marbella under the care of a high-risk pregnancy doctor. I was scared to stay in Nassau with my doctor because he had asked me to go on bedrest for the entire pregnancy. I couldn't imagine being stuck like that for the entire nine months. I was lucky that the Spanish doctor I had chosen was the best in the business, and he assured me that I could have a normal pregnancy if I was willing to take things a little easier. I'm glad that I met him and listened to his advice. On November 16, 2005, I gave birth to a baby boy, Daniel. I was a mother, and I was ecstatic. This amazing doctor ended up helping me with my next three pregnancies as well, and he even baptized my son. He and his wife were always supportive and there for me. We ended up being close friends.

I stayed in Marbella until Daniel was four weeks old, and then we returned to the Bahamas. For the next four years, I split my time between Marbella and the Bahamas, though I was mostly in Marbella. During this time, I had three more babies, Julien, Ella, and Isabella. I miscarried twice more in between my successful pregnancies. Each was sad, but I was more optimistic about pregnancy again after the help I received from my doctor.

Geneva, 2008

When Daniel was three and Ella was one, we decided to move to Switzerland. We moved to a small town called Versoix, which was about a ten-mile drive from Geneva. There, we enrolled Daniel at College De Limon, a good private international school. George hoped to open an office there so he would only need to leave occasionally for New York.

Living in Switzerland was hard for our family. In the beginning, George was only able come home every few weeks, and each trip was only a week long, ten days at the most. I found it hard to adjust with few friends there. I had trouble finding a pediatrician for the children as the system was different for new patients in Geneva. It depended on the area in which you lived, and the kids were getting sick. We had rented a large old house. Though it was nice, it had poor insulation. Every time the wind blew, we could feel it through the entire house. The heating system was very old, and most of the time it malfunctioned. It was always freezing inside, and the kids and I were always sick.

I had gotten pregnant again. My third. I was worried about finding a doctor in Geneva that I could trust as much as I did my doctor in Marbella, with whom I was constantly on the phone with going over my test results. Nor was I used to being in the cold after the perfect weather I had experienced in Marbella and the Bahamas.

Daniel was not adjusting well to his new school. Every day he cried and vomited. And I didn't like the Swiss people. Unlike folks in the Bahamas and in Marbella, the Swiss I met were unfriendly and kept their distance. After being there for five months, I had not met one nice person that I felt I could be friends with. Nor did any of the parents go to the park with their children. It was next to impossible to socialize and meet people.

My sisters and George's brother came to visit us at Christmas. We had an lovely time together, and I was very sad to see them leave. By March, I hated Switzerland. I felt it would be best to move back to Marbella, especially as a few of my pregnancy checks came back with strange results. Going back to Marbella cost us a fortune, but we were all happy and healthier being back in the sunshine.

Life was challenging with my babies, but it was worth it. Fortunately I had a lovely woman named Patricia who helped me with the children. On May 29, I gave birth to Julien. We moved from our apartment, which we kept and still have today, to a larger house for the three children, Patricia, George, and me. We lived in that beautiful home for a year. We also had a new lady from Romania to help me with the kids. Her name was Tita, and she adored Julien. She was with him constantly. She worked for us for about eighteen months, and then she had to return to Romania.

I was exhausted as Julien was a terrible sleeper and had bad reflux. If I moved him even slightly to the left or right, his food came back up. Thank God it stopped almost completely around fourteen months.

Daniel was four now and going to school. Again, we enrolled him in an international school called Aloha College for children from three to eighteen years of age. This time, he made friends and was happy in school. His best friend was a little boy from Syria. The two of them loved acting and singing and were inseparable the entire school year. Unfortunately, the little boy moved back to Syria, and our sons lost touch.

Ella started going to a small kindergarten, or *guarderia* as they called it in Spain. It was owned by two lovely ladies who took great care of the kids. Everyone was speaking Spanish. It was a private nursery for children between the ages of one and three. Although it was private, the price was very reasonable. We paid 120 euros per month. It had a very large garden and plenty of trees that gave the children shade during the day. In a corner of the garden there was a sandbox, and they had plenty of bicycles and tricycles for the kids. They spent at least 3 hours outside every day when the weather was nice.

To escape the heat during the summer months, they had a nice-size inflatable pool, and every child was allowed to go in for at least five minutes and play. Inside, they had a painting room and a real classroom, where every day they were taught algebra and the alphabet. The teachers brought snacks for the kids, and they did plenty of acting and dancing.

Ella went to kindergarten with a pair of twin boys. One day, one of the twins upset her, and she bit him. Instead of just biting the one, she bit both twins. When asked why she had bit both of them, she said, "Because I didn't know which one bit me, so I had to make sure I punish both of them." It wasn't good that she bit her friends, but her response made it a funny story. She was suspended from the school, and she stayed at home for a week because of it. Later, when Ella turned three, she went to Aloha like Daniel had.

Back to the Bahamas

George and I would see each other in Marbella for only ten days out of each month. When our youngest, Isabella, was born, we decided to move back to the Bahamas and live there full-time. Daniel and Ella had been attending a nice school in Marbella for two years when we made the decision to move. Kids began school early in Spain. The children were only three years old when they enrolled. After starting their education in so early, Daniel and Ella were both very knowledgeable when they got to school in Nassau. Daniel, now four, went to school very close to where we lived, and Ella went to a play school nearby. Julien stayed home with me.

Daniel was supposed to go to first grade, but because he was only four, they moved him to prekindergarten. Two weeks later, though, they moved him up to kindergarten at my insistence. He was already able to read and write and was so far ahead of his class. He had already gone through kindergarten in Spain, and I was unhappy with him repeating the grade because he was very bright.

I loved finally being back in the Bahamas even though I missed Spain. And we all missed George. In the Bahamas, he was able to come home every weekend. This was a better arrangement as the children were young and needed their father. We all also felt safer when George was with us.

We got settled in the Bahamas, and I looked up the few friends I had from when I lived there in 1997. I got in touch with them right away, and that made my return much easier.

While living in the Bahamas, I made every effort to approach other Romanians living there, and I met many people, all classy and fun. I love to entertain at home, so I would hold lovely dinners, and we would share our experiences from home and enjoy good quality time together. Debra, my sister-in-law, also came to the Bahamas many times to keep me company. Over the years, we had become very close. She had come to visit me for three months through my pregnancy with Daniel in Spain, so coming to visit in Nassau was an easy decision for her.

Over time, I met many other people who became dear to us in the Bahamas. Every Wednesday, my girlfriends and I and used to go out for girls' night. My friend Donna and her husband became my best friends. Donna accepted me as I was and has always made me feel wonderful. We are still in touch today, and our friendship is as strong as ever.

I am still especially close with friends Jen and Sara, whom I love and greatly respect. I also met an amazing woman named Dominique, from Quebec, who was a ball of energy and always ready for action. Our children became good friends, and we even went on vacation together. When she was on the island, Melinda, a very dear friend of mine originally from Russia, was always ready to go out and have a great time, and the two of us shared many wonderful nights out dancing and dining and celebrating life together. Another beautiful friend that I have shared amazing memories with is Jennifer, the godmother of two of my children. She helped us rebuild and design two of our homes over the years, and we spent a lot of time together not just in the Bahamas but in Marbella and in the US as well.

And I cannot forget one of my Romanian friends, Adina. When my father was on the beach one day in Nassau, just before our wedding, he was chatting with my sisters in Romanian. Adina was there with her daughter, and she approached them and said hello. We clicked right away and became good friends. We were very close for a while, but our friendship took a bit of break here and there over time. We still talk, but we're not as close as we used to be. Living on a small island has many social benefits, but there are some difficulties too. While it is easy to meet interesting people, make strong connections, and develop wonderful friendships, along with so much entertaining—there is always a party to go and adult life becomes a continuous playdate full of parties and fun—living on a small island comes with a price.

We were sometimes stuck with people we didn't especially enjoy. I saw the same people at the supermarket, the gym, the beach, and in restaurants. This meant we always had to be on our best behavior or we would lose our reputation and get trapped on an island with people snubbing their noses at us. Of course, that wasn't the case most of the time. Once in a while, we were very lucky to meet some wonderful people who we wanted to hang out with all the time.

And of course, because we lived on an island, everyone knew everything about everyone else. It reminded me of living in my grandmother's town back in Romania in that way. Sometimes people would make up stories if they didn't know someone that well. For this reason, there were times when I looked forward to leaving the island so I didn't have to be part of the clique anymore.

Though I felt safe with the children both in Marbella and in the Bahamas, two incidents occurred while George was away. In 2014, we were robbed in Marbella. The children and I were there for the summer. My in-laws were with us for a few weeks as well. We were in a shoe shop in the old town, where the children were trying on sandals. When I went to pay, my wallet was not in my bag. Someone had stolen it. I couldn't believe it. I hadn't even been aware of it happening. I had a very large amount of cash with me because a day later I was planning to travel to Rome with Daniel.

The children were scared and disappointed. "If Pappy were here, this never would have happened," they told me. It saddened me that they thought we were not protected unless he was with us. I never recovered the money, and the police never found the thief.

A year after that incident, I was in Marbella for the summer again, and I went to my local bank to discuss my bills with my bank manager. As I was waiting for her, two men entered the bank with masks over their faces. One of them held a gun and the other a large ax. There were three women there who worked for the bank, along with myself and an older gentleman. The man with the ax came straight over to me. He said if I stayed calm and quiet, nothing would happen to me. The other guy with the gun walked to the teller and told her to open the safe. We all stood in shock. One of the tellers started crying hysterically. The other one looked like she was close to fainting.

The manager told them that the teller didn't know the code because she was new there. The guy with the gun said he would shoot her and I would be next. All this time the man with the ax was standing over me, holding one hand on my shoulder and the other hand held the ax above my head. I was paralyzed with fear. Thank God the children weren't with me.

The bank manager opened the safe, and the men left after taking the money from inside, about four thousand euros in total. The police arrived a few minutes later. We all had to go to the station and give statements, which took a few hours. I left the police station shaken and crying, thinking just how short life can be. Every minute we have on this planet is precious. Unfortunately, this is easy to forget until death stares us in the face. I never heard back from the police or received an apology from the bank, but I was just glad to be alive. My children were very upset for a long time after I told them what happened.

In spite of these two incidents, we all still loved visiting in Marbella. The city has such a good vibe and an amazing energy. We considered these two incidents as just terrible coincidences.

In 2014, after we got back from our European trip, one night someone broke into our guest cottage in Nassau. They got in through a bathroom window. They took a TV and few other small items. We called the police in the morning, and two officers came, a lady and a man. They asked a couple of questions, and I was shocked to see that the female officer used her old cell phone to take pictures of the crime scene. Then she took out this small homemade-looking kit to take the fingerprints. It was ridiculously unprofessional. I had found the TV set on the side of the road couple hours later. Of course it was broken. Then about two months later, our car was stolen from the driveway. I used to leave my keys inside it. I just never thought that someone would drive away with it in the middle of the night because we lived in a safe community. The car was found inside our community again two hours later. The thieves weren't able to drive it out because they were stopped at the gate. They left the car and ran. Although these were serious incidents, fortunately they are the only bad memories we have of safety issues in either country.

Travels

I am a hyperenergetic person and always need to be busy. Before I go to bed, I like to have a plan for the next day. Fortunately, having three children met this need as I was kept constantly busy with school, swimming lessons, and other activities, along with socializing with my friends and theirs.

In the summers, I always took the children to Marbella, Italy, or France. Having been born in Marbella, they associated Spain with home and enjoyed going there the most and as often as we could. George would come for a week here and there whenever he was able to get out of work.

It was hard for him because he was alone and away from me and the kids. I felt lonely without him, too, and often overworked myself by trying to keep the kids busy. I took them to different camps for around four hours a day. They had a good time but missed their father greatly.

When we decided to buy our house in the Bahamas, I was on vacation in Europe and had to go to Positano, Italy, in order to sign the papers for the house because my Bahamian lawyer happened to be there on vacation too. This was back in the summer of 2004. Luckily, my very good friend Sara, who was in England at the time, decided to meet me in Rome, and we traveled down to Positano together for a week and then went on to Capri. We had the most amazing time together in Italy, and I treasure the beautiful memories we made.

In December 2010, I gave birth to my fourth child, Isabella. My doctor advised that I tie my tubes at the same time. Though I would no longer be able to get pregnant, except through in vitro surgery, and after much thought, we decided to go ahead with the procedure because of all the bleeding during my pregnancy with her.

As it turned out, Isabella was a twin, but the other baby never made it. This was confirmed during my caesarean. I had bled throughout the pregnancy with the uterus's attempt to clean out the other baby. This made me very sad. I always wanted to have twins, and I had had two chances, but neither worked out. Unfortunately, it was not meant to be.

I deeply regretted having my tubes tied. I felt a part of me was not the same, like I wasn't good enough anymore. To have a baby through in vitro was too much for me emotionally, and after three years I finally let go of the thought of having another baby.

In the summer of 2011, while I was in Europe on vacation with the kids, George started a new extension of our house. He told me that by the time I got back in two months, it should be done. Of course, when I returned, it wasn't. We had to move in to a rental house. The rental house was in the same community as ours, so I was able to go and check on the construction daily. I was there every single day for hours making sure everything they did was on time and done correctly. I was also in a mad rush, as always, about moving in. Every month we had to pay rent, and the owners of the house told us that if we were not out by Thanksgiving, we would be charged a higher price. The rental house was around five thousand square feet and smaller than our house today, but the prices would still increase drastically over the holidays.

I was on a mission to move in to our own home as soon as it was close to acceptable. When I finally moved in, we had just one bathroom working upstairs. In the night, we had to take turns putting all four kids in the bath and using the toilet. Covered in dust, we had workers around us all the time, and even today I don't know why I did not stay in the rental house until it was done. If it hadn't been for the high price to rent, we should have stayed there until the construction was over. It was a nightmare for the first two weeks, but it worked out in the end. The construction was finished by the end of November, and it turned out beautifully as my friend Jennifer had created such wonderful plans for the house. We now had three more bedrooms and a very large hallway. I felt so happy to finally be living in it.

Something amazing came out of doing more construction to extend the house. Patricia was working for us and then Victoria too. We had hired Victoria that summer after returning from Europe. Our old housekeeper had left, and Victoria was young, bubbly, energetic, and always in a good mood. Both Patricia and Victoria were from the same city in Romania, and now our house was bigger, we had space to give both wonderful ladies room in our home. Victoria was a big help, especially with Isabella, who was just nine months when we moved to the new house. Unfortunately, Victoria left after six months. She fell in love with the electrical engineer at my house while it had been under construction, and they were planning on getting married. I was happy for her but sad to see her leave, though we still saw her from time to time. We lost a beautiful person, but she gained a wonderful life.

Life Today in Florida

Throughout our marriage, my illegal status was always in the background. Everything we did, every decision we made, was connected to my return to the US. Though many lawyers, politicians, and influential people tried desperately to help us, I felt constantly frustrated. My sisters kept coming and going so easily. George was coming and going sometimes twice in a week, but I was always stuck.

I felt guilty about the stress this put on George to make things happen. Despairing that our dreams would never happen, I wanted us to stop trying to get back to the US and make our home somewhere else. We had many arguments about this. I wanted him to find a job in Europe so we could live together happily as a normal family. In all the years we had been together, we had never spent one whole month together, and he was deprived of spending time with his children. We both felt this strain on our relationship.

But he was in a high position in his company, and he had worked there for twenty years. He didn't want to give it up. If he transferred to Europe, he would have to start again from the bottom with considerably less pay. I felt I was keeping him from succeeding professionally.

In the end, George finally got me back into the US. He promised from the first date we had in that restaurant that he would take care of me. He would make me happy, marry me, and give me a life that would always keep me busy and inspired. And though it took a long time and was very hard for both of us, it finally happened.

After leaving the US in 2003, I was finally permitted back in 2015, twelve years after I had left. It hadn't been easy. We had three sets of lawyers and many interviews with the American Embassy. I had three interviews in Madrid and three more in Nassau. This took a lot of money and caused so much stress for us that it almost cost us our marriage too. Thank God we made it through.

On April 15, 2015, we had our interview for a green card at the Embassy in Nassau. George was a US citizen, so the children and I were finally granted green cards. The nightmare was finally over, and there was new hope for our family and our marriage. So much stress had been lifted from our shoulders at last—just like *that*. It felt heavenly.

I came to New York to celebrate with George just a few days after I got my green card. I met up with my sisters and brothers-in-law, and we all went out. It felt incredible to walk around the city of Manhattan again and to make plans and see my friends I had not seen in twelve years. I was free again, and we had to start making new arrangements for our upcoming life in the US with our children.

George's office moved from New York to West Palm Beach, Florida, and today we live just a drive away, in Boca Raton, with our four children. George has a relatively short commute back and forth to the office every day, but it's nothing compared to flying across the world to see us like he used to.

We bought a new family car and started looking to rent a home at first. After we rented for six months, we decided to buy a home. It took me just two months looking around with a realtor, and I fell in love with our house before I even saw it. As soon as I entered the gates of the community, I was mesmerized. As we drove to the house, I prayed hard that I would like the house too. Luckily, I did. Just like when we bought our house in the Bahamas, this house felt like our home right away. The drive to school for the kids was only ten minutes or so, and slowly we started feeling comfortable in this new country.

The kids are flourishing. Daniel is eleven, Ella is nine, Julien is seven, and the youngest, Isabella, is six. Parenting four children is a challenge, but they are all great kids who, although they look alike, differ in character and make everything worthwhile.

Daniel is intelligent and sensitive. A copy of his father, he loves to read and be in touch with what's going on in politics, sports, and entertainment. But he is also disorganized and lazy, and we do get into arguments. For instance, we will argue about him feeling that he speaks French very well, which he learned in Geneva, though actually he remembers very little. I always support him though and say, "It's been a long time, baby. It's okay to forget."

Ella is a very bright and determined girl and the artist of the house. She loves to sing, dance, act, and do gymnastics. She's always trying to perfect her cartwheels or handstands.

Julien is our blue-eyed, charming, and mischievous child with a contagious smile. Always ready to help me or his father with some housework, he is quite responsible for his age.

Isabella, the youngest, is a nice polite, sweet girl—when she wants to be! She is mature for her age, and her conversations are more like those of a ten-year-old. Right now, she is going through a phase where her response to everything is, "I don't want to." She's trying to copy her older siblings, I guess.

I am trying my best to raise well-behaved, responsible, educated children, but taking care of four children close in age is hectic and demanding, and there's often a lot of chaos and stress. They always fight, argue, shout, and disagree, and I guess they will continue no matter their age.

Life today is so different to the way I was raised. It can be a tremendous challenge as our children have more than they need and are overloaded with information. It can be good to have so much, but it also erodes the parental influence, and that makes it hard on me and George. For instance, we need to explain to them constantly why they can't have or do certain things whenever they want or feel like it. This often makes them angry. I think that our society today makes children very needy. They are always told that they can do whatever they please or they can be whomever they want. I understand that this empowers them and makes them feel invincible. I like that part, but this also makes them spoiled and privileged. If we tell them not to do something, their answer is always, "Why not?" They have no shame in arguing with us about what they want or how they feel even though we make our intentions clear. When I was a kid, I was very scared to argue or debate with my parents. Once my parents told me no, that was it. Not these children of today's generation, though. I really don't like the lack of respect many children have for their parents, grandparents, teachers, or older people today. It's something I struggle with on a daily basis. George works very hard to provide us with a good lifestyle, and they get upset sometimes when he can't come to certain school events. We explain to them that there is work time and there's playtime, and unfortunately, sometimes he cannot be with us.

In our house, I am the general who disciplines the children, and George is the nice, calm daddy, ready to play and listen. He is patient and positive, while I sometimes have an insane temper, exploding at the drop of a hat. Like the Italians, I gesture with my hands when I talk, and my voice rises. I always calm down a few minutes later. All in all, this makes us a good team and creates balance in our household. I am working on trying to incorporate better energy and positivity in my parenting. I wish that I had had the children when I was younger so I could have more energy to play with them as I always feel exhausted. I was thirty-three when I had Daniel, thirty-five with Ella, thirty-six with Julien, and Isabella was my Christmas baby when I was thirty-seven. And with four of them all close in age, no wonder I'm exhausted!

George comes from a family of teachers, and education reigns supreme in our house. We try to expose them to the world at large. From an early age, our kids were lucky to have traveled the world so much. In addition to living in Spain, Switzerland, and the Bahamas, as well as many trips to Romania, Daniel came with us to Prague and Vienna when he was just three, though of course he doesn't remember this. We also try to go to England and Ireland once every other year to visit George's parents and his brother and sister-in-law. We always go to Marbella as our first destination in the summer. It's our base in Europe. From there, we take shorter trips for a week or so to different destinations all through Europe. George joins us sometimes, and when he can't, we go without him. Even without George, I always have Patricia with me. During the school year, we go away at Christmas or sometimes for Easter. At the same time, we try to impress upon the children how fortunate they are to be able to travel the way we do.

I try to be the best mother I can be, but I get easily stressed and fly off the handle. I've gained much insight as to the causes of my ill temper. Of course, it has a lot to do with the way I was raised. There was always a shortage of money, love, care, and affection while I was growing up. My parents were cold and practical—"You need to do this." "You don't need that," they would say. We missed out on after-school activities like tennis, gymnastics, piano, or ballet. We had asked but my parents always said no. They told us that we needed to concentrate on doing homework and housework. But in truth, there was neither the money nor the time for all the activities we wanted to try.

My father was a negative person. He still is very negative in every area of his life. When he comes to visit or stay with me, we always end up arguing. I can't believe we are related sometimes. He is always ready to say no to anything even before there's a chance to explain what you mean. I know him well, but after a while he just gets on my nerves. I am so happy George doesn't understand much Romanian most of the time because the two of them get along just perfectly. The secret really is that neither of them speak the same language as the other.

My mother was always stressed when we were growing up because she had no money to buy us new uniforms or other basic school essentials. When we complained, she called us ungrateful children, and we fought constantly. As a stressed-out parent, I can now understand more about why they were this way.

In addition to all my parenting responsibilities, I enjoy taking yoga classes and just got my certification to teach. In 2015, just after being granted my green card to the US, my very good friend Dawn and I went on a yoga retreat in Mexico. The retreat was a week long, but after three days I couldn't stay there anymore. Part of the retreat involved doing a lot of opening up about emotions and feelings, and this was hard for me.

The resort was also a bit too close to nature for me. There were no real walls or windows in the rooms, just a roof. We were practically outside, the ambience of which, I believe, was supposed to help us open up. But I found it hard to sleep, and though the place was beautiful, I broke down and felt I had had enough and had to leave. Even though Dawn was able to handle it all very well, she's such as amazing friend that she left with me back to return to Miami. I remain ever grateful to her for sticking up for me and truly being when I needed her.

But becoming at yoga teacher has helped me in my practice in becoming more spiritual. I am more in touch with my emotions and feelings, something I have always struggled with. Though I've never been an open person, even with my husband, I want to change. I feel I am making more progress on this goal now. Just recently, I started teaching classes, and I am enjoying this new chapter of my life very much. I teach part-time now just because I don't want to interfere with my time with the children. I know one day this will become my life. Teaching is very fulfilling, and I am looking forward to finishing another teaching course in a year from now to see where it takes me.

George has put up with a lot. Thank God he is calm and calculated and reasons with me. Still, it's been challenging for us to make good decisions about everyday life. Of course, now with our family, it's not just me and him. We are responsible for these little people we brought into this world. To do right by them, we have to make every effort to behave like responsible adults. At the same time, both of us still remain children inside to some extent and all the responsibility can be scary. There are so many times we just want to give up, but we always choose not to.

Having come from different countries, different cultures, and speaking different languages, I am sometimes amazed that our marriage survived. But it has. Though I feel I explain myself well in English, the two of us still encounter many misunderstandings. We work on communicating better daily and we make every attempt to listen to each other.

Though I love my life in Boca Raton, I miss my special and beautiful friends from the Bahamas. While I love the privacy I have here and the feeling of living in a small city, I miss being close to the beautiful Bahamian beaches and especially the Old Fort club, where we spent many weekends together having a great time in the early stages of our marriage. I also miss the very modern club, Albany, which was always a wonderful breath of fresh air for us. Exclusive clubs like this are impossible to find in Boca, so every few months we go back to Nassau to see our friends and have fun.

So while I enjoy a great life today living in Florida, I can't help but miss both Marbella and Nassau, where we spent twelve years of our life going back and forth. I'm also grateful that today Nassau has more conveniences than it did in 2003 when I lived there, supermarkets and more shops, making life much easier on the island for my friends.

All in all, my life is great, and I am very grateful to have such a wonderful family. Twenty-five years ago, I never would have dreamed my life would turn out to be so wonderful and fulfilling. George and I have been married for sixteen years now, and the entire time we've been together, he has always been my biggest supporter. This book, which for many years was just a dinner conversation, wouldn't have happened if he had not been here to support me. Thank you, my dear husband, for being a wonderful father, friend, lover, and husband. My life is a blessing, and I am very grateful for it all.

ABOUT THE AUTHOR

Mirela Gasan is a mother of four and a certified yoga instructor. She teaches yoga in her spare time near her home in Boca Raton, Florida. She also enjoys taking classes as often as she can. Currently she is planning to open her own yoga studio. She loves reading and has very much enjoyed writing this book.

Printed in the USA
CFSIA information can be obtained
at www.ICGtesting.com
LVHW090009221023
761657LV00053B/611